PENGUIN REFERENCE

The Penguin Dictionary of English Grammar

R. L. Trask was born in western New York State in 1944. For some years he pursued a career in chemistry in the USA and in Turkey. In 1970 he came to England and switched to linguistics, obtaining his Ph.D. from the University of London in 1983. He taught linguistics at the University of Liverpool from 1979 to 1988, since when he has taught in the School of Cognitive and Computing Sciences at the University of Sussex. His special interests are historical linguistics, grammar and the Basque language. He is the author of a number of books, including *A Dictionary of Grammatical Terms in Linguistics*, *Language Change*, *Language: The Basics*, *A Dictionary of Phonetics and Phonology*, *Historical Linguistics*, *The History of Basque*, *The Penguin Guide to Punctuation* and *Mind the Gaffe*.

The Penguin Dictionary of

English Grammar

R. L. Trask

PENGUIN BOOKS

PENGUIN BOOKS

Published by the Penguin Group
Penguin Books Ltd, 80 Strand, London WC2 ORL, England
Penguin Putnam Inc., 375 Hudson Street, New York, New York 10014, USA
Penguin Books Australia Ltd, Ringwood, Victoria, Australia
Penguin Books Canada Ltd, 10 Alcorn Avenue, Toronto, Ontario, Canada M4V 3B2
Penguin Books India (P) Ltd, 11, Community Centre, Panscheel Park,
New Delhi – 110 017, India
Penguin Books (NZ) Ltd, Cnr Rosedale and Airborne Roads,
Albany, Auckland, New Zealand
Penguin Books (South Africa) (Pty) Ltd, 24 Sturdee Avenue, Rosebank 2196, South Africa

Penguin Books Ltd, Registered Offices: 80 Strand, London WC2 ORL, England

www.penguin.com

First published 2000

7

Set in ITC Stone
Typeset by Rowland Phototypesetting Ltd, Bury St Edmunds, Suffolk
Printed in England by Clays Ltd, St Ives plc

Preface

GRAMMAR is the study of word structure and sentence structure. Grammar has been pursued for centuries, and a number of different approaches have been developed and elaborated. These approaches differ to some extent in the analyses they recognize, and, inevitably, they differ also in their terminology.

Many of the most venerable traditional terms are still in use today, such as ADJECTIVE, TRANSITIVE VERB, DIRECT OBJECT and RELATIVE CLAUSE. Other traditional terms are now obsolete or at least old-fashioned, such as SUBSTANTIVE and NOUN CLAUSE. At the same time, important new terms, not used by our ancestors, have been introduced into the subject and have become indispensable; examples are DETERMINER, NOUN PHRASE, COMPLEMENT CLAUSE and SUBJECT RAISING.

Such change in terminology is natural and inevitable in any field of study. However, the existence today of several quite distinct approaches to the study of grammar has the unappealing consequence that grammarians of different persuasions use somewhat different terminology. For example, the proponents of transformational grammar attach great importance to the concepts they call DEEP STRUCTURE and SURFACE STRUCTURE, which are not even recognized in other approaches. And the authors of the QUIRK GRAMMARS of English employ a collection of innovating names for labelling types of adverbial, such as SUBJUNCT and ADJUNCT, terms used by no one else for this purpose.

Worse still, different grammarians sometimes use the same term in quite different senses. Examples of this include ADJUNCT, PARTICLE, CONJUNCT and COMPLEMENT, terms which can denote rather different things depending upon who is using them.

Irritating though it may be, this variation in terminology is not vast. Most grammarians today use much the same terminology as other grammarians, and the differences in usage are only an exasperating little nuisance, not a formidable obstacle to understanding.

The purpose of this book is to introduce our present-day grammatical terminology as clearly as possible. Virtually every significant term is entered and explained, usually with some examples to illustrate the use of the term. Competing and conflicting usages are carefully explained, and there are numerous cross-references to related terms.

This book treats only the terminology of grammar. Terms pertaining to the study of other areas of language, such as pronunciation, meaning and history, are not covered here. Punctuation is included, but only in its main points; for more detailed information, see *The Penguin Guide to Punctuation*. The focus throughout is on the grammar of English, but the dictionary nevertheless includes grammatical terms which are chiefly important in the grammatical study of other languages, such as ABLATIVE and GENDER.

R. L. Trask

A

abbreviation A brief way of writing a word or a phrase that could also be written out in full, using only the letters of the alphabet and possibly full stops. Examples are *Dr* for *Doctor, Prof.* for *Professor, Capt.* for *Captain* and *lx* for *linguistics*. In British usage, an abbreviation that contains the first and last letters of the full expression, like *Dr,* does not take a full stop; in American usage, it does, and *Dr.* is preferred. Many abbreviations are derived from Latin equivalents for English words and phrases, such as *lb.* for *pound(s), e.g.* for *for example, i.e.* for *in other words* and *et al.* for *and others*. An abbreviation does not normally have a distinct pronunciation of its own: we pronounce *Dr* as 'Doctor' and *e.g.* as 'for example'. But there are exceptions: the abbreviation *p.* for *pence* is sometimes pronounced 'pee'. However, saying 'ee-jee' for *e.g.* or 'eye-ee' for *i.e.* is eccentric. Some people extend the term 'abbreviation' to include ACRONYMS and INITIALISMS, but this use is neither usual nor recommended. An abbreviation must be distinguished from a clipped form (see under CLIPPING), which is not an abbreviation but a real word, and from a LOGOGRAM, which is not constructed from letters of the alphabet.

ablative In a language with CASE, a particular case-form which denotes 'from', 'away from' and sometimes also 'out of'. An example is Basque *-tik*: attached to *etxe,* 'house', this gives *etxetik*, 'from the house, away from the house, out of the house'. Note that the 'ablative' case of Latin has a variety of miscellaneous uses, of which 'ablative' in the strict sense is only one: for example, it serves to provide the objects of most prepositions and to provide ABSOLUTE CONSTRUCTIONS in that language.

absolute comparative A COMPARATIVE form used with no standard of comparison: *Whizzo washes whiter; the younger generation*. That is, there is no answer provided to questions like 'Whiter than what?' or 'Younger than who?'

absolute construction (also **nominative absolute**) A phrase which is linked to the sentence containing it only by meaning and intonation, with no grammatical link of any kind. In the following examples, the bracketed sequences are absolute constructions: [*The day being cloudy,*] *we decided to stay home*; *The two women* [*, their business concluded,*] *retired to the bar*. Compare the example *The two women, having concluded their business, retired to the bar*, in which the phrase enclosed in commas *is* overtly linked to the rest of the sentence by the participle *having*.

absolute transitive A label sometimes applied to a VERB which can appear in the construction called UNSPECIFIED OBJECT DELETION.

abstract noun A NOUN which denotes something which is not physical and cannot be touched, such as *happiness*, *absence*, *advice*, *beauty* or *history*. Sometimes the term is extended to include nouns denoting events and actions, such as *arrival*, *explosion* and *somersault*. Compare CONCRETE NOUN.

acceptability The degree to which a linguistic form is considered normal, usable and comprehensible by speakers. Acceptability judgements arise in at least three circumstances. First, speakers of differing geographical, social and educational backgrounds may genuinely differ in what they regard as normal and acceptable. Here are a few examples of variably acceptable pieces of English; the per cent sign indicates that what follows is normal and acceptable to some speakers but not to others: % *You need your hair cutting*; % *It ain't funny*; % *You have to really give it a go*; % *This road is terrible any more*; % *We have agreed a deal*; % *Having said that, there's another option*; % *This paper was written by Mike and myself*. Second, some pieces of English 'stretch' the ordinary rules to the point at which many speakers find it difficult to decide whether or not they are normal: % *Susie was seen by the students while enjoying themselves*; % *There's the woman that I didn't know if she was coming or not*; % *I phoned the woman that I met at the party up*. Third, certain pieces of English which clearly conform to the rules of English grammar present serious difficulties for mental processing, and may therefore be rejected: % *The book the professor the students who failed their exam complained about is hard to understand* (this means 'The book which the professor who the students who failed their exam complained about is hard to understand'); % *The horse shot from the stable collapsed* (this means 'The horse which was shot from the stable collapsed'); % *Flounder flounder badger badger flounder* (this last means '[Flounder which [other] flounder badger] [[themselves] badger [other] flounder]').

accidence An old-fashioned term for INFLECTION, now little used.

accusative In a language with CASE, a particular case-form which serves to mark the DIRECT OBJECT of a verb. For example, the Latin noun *puella*, 'girl', has the accusative form *puellam*, as in *Puellam vidit*, 'I saw the girl'. In Latin and some other case languages, the accusative also has some further miscellaneous functions. The label *accusative* is sometimes applied to the OBJECTIVE case of English, but this is not really appropriate, since the English objective case serves a large number of functions, of which the direct object is only one.

accusative and infinitive The traditional name for a certain construction, found in English and in some other languages, in which a verb is followed by a NOUN PHRASE in the OBJECTIVE or ACCUSATIVE case and an INFINITIVE – in English, an infinitive preceded by *to*. Examples: *She wants me to come home; I persuaded them to wait a little longer; Her coach advised her to work on her serve.*

acronym In the simplest case, a word constructed by combining the initial letters of the principal words in a phrase to produce something which can be pronounced as a word and which has the same meaning as the original phrase. Examples include *scuba* for *self-contained underwater breathing apparatus*, *laser* for *light amplification by the stimulated emission of radiation* and *NATO* for *North Atlantic Treaty Organization*. Some acronyms depart from the canonical pattern in various ways, such as *radar* for *radio detection and ranging*. Some people extend the term *acronym* to an INITIALISM, which is formed in the same way but cannot be pronounced as a word, such as *BBC*.

active voice The characteristic of a verb-form, or of the clause containing it, whose SUBJECT represents the ACTOR, the person or thing presented as most directly responsible for the action or state denoted by the verb. In English, an INTRANSITIVE verb can only appear in the active voice: *The sun rose at 6.30 this morning*; *Susie smiled knowingly*. A TRANSITIVE verb most commonly occurs in the active voice: *The Mongols sacked Baghdad*; *Susie wrote this book*; *We are eating our dinner*; *Mike will collect our clothes from the dry cleaner*. In all these cases, the subject (the noun phrase at the beginning of the sentence) represents the person or thing responsible for the action. But, by choosing our verb appropriately, we can sometimes present either of two entities as responsible for the action or state: *The play delighted Susie* means about the same as *Susie enjoyed the play*, but the first presents *the play* as the source of the enjoyment, while the second presents *Susie* in that role, yet both sentences are in the active voice. Compare PASSIVE VOICE.

actor A generalization of the concept of an AGENT to include any person or thing that is presented as chiefly responsible for the action or state denoted by a sentence. In all of the following sentences, *Susie* is an actor, but *Susie* is an agent only in the first: *Susie washed the car*; *Susie received a letter*; *Susie dreamt about Mike*; *Susie weighs 55 kilos*; *Susie earns over £30,000*; *Susie has blue eyes*.

adjectival A label applied to any word, phrase or other linguistic item which modifies a NOUN in the way that an ADJECTIVE does. In the following examples, the bold italic item is adjectival; *my **new** book* (an adjective phrase consisting only of an adjective); *a **very long** opera* (an adjective phrase containing a degree modifier and an adjective); *the roses **in your garden*** (a prepositional phrase); *a **copper-producing** region* (a participial phrase); *his **damn-your-eyes** attitude* (an entire sentence reduced to a modifier); *the woman **you were talking to*** (a relative clause). A few linguists would also apply the label *adjectival* to a noun modifying another noun, as in *a **security** van* and *a **plastic** cup*, but this use is not normal.

adjectival passive The PASSIVE PARTICIPLE of a verb functioning as an ADJECTIVAL, sometimes accompanied by additional modifiers. In the following examples, the bold italic sequences are adjectival passives: *a **newly discovered** fossil*; ***well-taught** children*; *a **ruined** city*; *an **uninhabited** island*. Most examples, like those just cited, involve the participles of TRANSITIVE verbs, but INTRANSITIVE verbs can also form adjectival passives: *a **vanished** civilization; their **long-departed** spirits.*

adjective The PART OF SPEECH that includes words like *big, happy, beautiful, interesting* and *sudden.* An adjective typically modifies a NOUN and denotes a temporary or permanent quality: for example, *a beautiful picture* is a picture which is distinguished from other pictures by being (permanently) beautiful, and *an exhausted player* is a player who is distinguished from other players by being (temporarily) exhausted. But this is not a definition, and some adjectives are different: for example, the adjective *mere,* as in *a mere child,* does not denote a quality of the child; the adjective *heavy,* when used as in *a heavy smoker,* does not denote a quality of the smoker, but rather of her habit; and the phrase *a counterfeit dollar* does not denote any kind of dollar at all, but only something designed to resemble a dollar, even though *counterfeit* is still an adjective.

A typical adjective exhibits the following properties:

1. It can be used in ATTRIBUTIVE position, as in *a(n)* __ *book.*

2. It can be used in PREDICATE position, as in *This book is* __.

3. It can be compared either with *-er, -est* or with *more, most; big, bigger, biggest; beautiful, more beautiful, most beautiful.*

4. It can take a DEGREE MODIFIER: *very big, too big, rather big, so big, exceedingly big.*

Many adjectives, however, fail to exhibit some of these properties, such as *awake, chief, topmost* and *final,* but these are still adjectives, because the properties that they do exhibit are typical adjective properties.

Note carefully that an English NOUN can also appear in attributive position, but in this position it remains a noun and does not become an adjective. For example, *red, short* and *expensive* are adjectives, in *a red dress, a short dress* and *an expensive dress,* but *cotton, maternity* and *cocktail* are nouns in *a cotton dress, a maternity dress* and *a cocktail dress.* Note the following differences, where an asterisk marks an ungrammatical expression: *This dress is expensive,* but **This dress is maternity; a more expensive dress,* but **a more maternity dress; a very expensive dress,* but **a very maternity dress.* Like adjectives, nouns can appear in attributive position, but they do not exhibit the other properties of adjectives.

adjective clause Another term for RELATIVE CLAUSE, now little used.

adjective phrase (AP) A PHRASE constructed around an ADJECTIVE as its HEAD. Examples: *as clever as Jan* (head adjective *clever*), *bigger than Chicago* (*bigger*), *very interesting* (*interesting*), *not sober enough to drive* (*sober*). A bare adjective, like *big* in *a big meal*, is also an adjective phrase, one consisting of the head adjective and no other material. Compare ADJECTIVAL.

adjunct **1**. Any part of a sentence which could in principle be removed without leaving behind something which is ungrammatical. An adjunct is always an ADVERBIAL of some kind. In the sentence *I ran into Susie in town yesterday*, the phrases *in town* and *yesterday* are adjuncts, since either or both could be removed without producing ungrammaticality, but nothing else is an adjunct, since removing anything else would produce an ungrammatical result. Compare ARGUMENT.

2. In the QUIRK GRAMMARS, an adverbial forming part of the structure of its clause, such as the examples just given. In these grammars, the term contrasts with CONJUNCT, DISJUNCT and SUBJUNCT.

adnominal A label applied to any element which modifies or determines the HEAD noun within a NOUN PHRASE. In the example *that rather nice bottle of wine we had at Susie's*, the determiner *that*, the adjective phrase *rather nice*, the prepositional phrase *of wine* and the relative clause *we had at Susie's* are all adnominal elements attached to the head noun *bottle*.

adposition Any item which is either a PREPOSITION or a POSTPOSITION.

adverb The PART OF SPEECH containing words like *slowly, happily, suddenly, here, tomorrow, soon* and *elsewhere*. An adverb usually modifies a VERB or a VERB PHRASE and provides information about the manner, time, place or circumstances of the activity or state denoted by the verb or verb phrase.

Adverbs are traditionally divided into three classes according to the kind of meaning they have, though this classification has nothing to do with their grammatical behaviour. A MANNER ADVERB says something about the manner in which an action is performed (*carefully, eagerly*); most of these end in *-ly*, but a few don't, such as the *fast* of *Susie drives too fast* and the very formal *thus*, as in *She did it thus*. A TIME ADVERB says something about the time of an action: *yesterday, soon, often, always, never*. A PLACE ADVERB says something about the location or direction of an action: *here, somewhere, elsewhere, uphill, ahead*.

Most adverbs of manner can be modified by DEGREE MODIFIERS: *very slowly, rather carefully, too fast, quite suddenly*. And most adverbs of manner can also be compared with *more* and *most* (rarely with *-er, -est*): *more carefully, most commonly, faster*. Most other adverbs do not accept degree modifiers or comparison, but a few do: *quite soon, very often, more often*.

Traditional grammarians, who worked with too few parts of speech, had the bad habit of applying the label *adverb* to almost any word that gave them trouble, including degree modifiers, PARTICLES and a number of rather miscellaneous words of doubtful category. Most linguists no longer do this, but some dictionaries and other reference books continue this practice; therefore, when your dictionary tells you that some word is an 'adverb', you should be a little cautious about accepting this at face value.

English has a rather distinctive subclass of adverbs called SENTENCE ADVERBS, which function rather differently from ordinary adverbs.

adverbial A functional label applied to any linguistic item, of whatever category, that behaves like an ADVERB with respect to the rest of its sentence. An adverbial may be an ADVERB PHRASE (including a bare adverb), a BARE-NP ADVERBIAL, a PREPOSITIONAL PHRASE, an ADVERBIAL CLAUSE or a NON-FINITE VERB PHRASE. In the following example, each of the bracketed sequences is an adverbial: *Susie confessed to me* [*rather unhappily*] *that she would have to go* [*to London*] [*this week*] [*to see her solicitor*] [*because there are problems with her contract*]. In the *QUIRK GRAMMARS, adverbials are classified into CONJUNCTS (sense 2), DISJUNCTS (sense 2), ADJUNCTS (sense 2) and SUBJUNCTS.*

adverbial clause (also **adverb clause)** Any SUBORDINATE CLAUSE which behaves as an ADVERBIAL with respect to the rest of its sentence. An adverbial clause may express time, place, manner, cause, purpose, concession, condition or another circumstance. In the examples below, the adverbial clauses are bracketed.

Time: [*As soon as she finished work,*] *Susie rushed off to play bridge; Let's have a drink* [*before we go*]; *I've been sleeping better* [*since I changed jobs.*]

Place: *Susie takes her mobile phone* [*wherever she goes.*]
Manner: *Susie drives* [*better than Mike does.*]
Cause: *I missed my flight* [*because my train was late.*]
Circumstance: [*Since Monday is a holiday,*] *let's take a day trip.*
Concession: [*Even though it had been raining for days,*] *the cricket pitch was in perfect condition*; *We're out of rice,* [*though we do have some pasta.*]
Condition: [*If Susie gets back in time,*] *she can go with us.*

Some of these types are often given distinctive names, such as TEMPORAL (for time), CIRCUMSTANTIAL, CONCESSIVE or CONDITIONAL clauses.

adverbial participle An ADVERBIAL headed by a PARTICIPLE: one type of NON-FINITE VERB PHRASE. In the following examples, the bracketed sequences are adverbial participles: [*Encouraged by her success,*] *she persevered*; [*Arriving a little early,*] *I decided to take a stroll.*

adverb phrase (AdvP) A PHRASE built around an ADVERB as its HEAD. An adverb phrase functions in a sentence in much the same way as an adverb, and the simplest type of adverb phrase is in fact a bare adverb. Examples of adverb phrases are *slowly, now, very soon, rather hurriedly* and *as gracefully as a cheetah.*

adverb preposing The construction in which an ADVERB occurs at the beginning of its sentence, instead of inside the VERB PHRASE. Examples: *Carefully she decanted the wine*; *Suddenly she burst into laughter*; *Nervously she lit a cigarette.*

AdvP The abbreviation for ADVERB PHRASE.

affirmative The opposite of NEGATIVE. The label is most commonly applied to a statement which contains no negative item, such as *There are rings around Jupiter* and *Susie sipped her brandy*, but it might equally be applied to questions and commands containing no negative, such as *Are you coming to Mike's party?* and *Wash your hands!*

affix A BOUND MORPHEME which is grammatical in nature. Affixes are classified according to the position they occupy. A PREFIX precedes the stem it is attached to, like the *un-* of *unhappy*, while a SUFFIX follows its stem, like the past-tense marker *-ed* in *walked*. See these entries for more examples. In some languages, more unusual types of affix exist, such as INFIXES. The addition of an affix to a word is *affixation*.

agent The SEMANTIC ROLE borne by the (typically human) entity that is the conscious and deliberate instigator of an action. Not every sentence contains an agent, but, if an agent is present, then, in English, it must normally be the SUBJECT. For example, *Susie* is an agent in each of the following: *Susie put up the shelves; Susie lit a cigarette; Susie slapped Mike; Susie wrote this book*. If an agent is present but is not the subject, then we must use the PASSIVE VOICE and precede the agent with *by*, as in *This book was written by Susie*. See also PATIENT.

In cases like *Susie spilled her wine* (assuming the spilling was not deliberate), *Susie fell asleep* and *Susie dreamt about Mike, Susie* is not an agent, because the actions are not deliberate. It is for cases like these that the superordinate term ACTOR has been introduced.

agentless passive See under PASSIVE VOICE.

agglutination Building a word by combining MORPHEMES into sequences without altering the forms of those morphemes. Agglutination occurs to a certain extent in English. For example, starting with the morpheme *happy*, we can attach first the prefix *un-* to obtain *unhappy* and then the suffix *-ness* to obtain *unhappiness*. Ignoring its pointless spelling change, this last word exhibits all three morphemes in clear and unaltered form, and this is agglutination. Other examples of agglutination in English are *dog-catchers* (*dog* plus *catch* plus *-er* plus *-s*) and *baby-sitting* (*baby* plus *sit* plus *-ing*). But most English words with multiple morphemes are not constructed in such a simple way; instead, the morphemes undergo various changes of shape: for example, *child* plus *-s* yields *children*; *take* plus *-ed* yields *took*; *photograph* plus *-y* yields *photography*; *electric* plus *-ity* yields *electricity*; *destroy* plus *-(t)ion* yields *destruction* (pay attention to the pronunciation, not to the spelling).

In some languages, such as Turkish, Japanese and Swahili, almost all words are constructed by agglutination, and we call these agglutinating languages. In others, such as Latin, French, Russian and the Eskimo languages, agglutination is almost unknown, and most words are formed in the messy way illustrated by the last English examples above. Compare INFLECTION.

agreement (also **concord**) The grammatical phenomenon in which the *form* of a particular word or phrase is determined by the *form* of another word or phrase which is grammatically linked with it. For example, English requires *this book* but *these books*: the form of the determiner *this/these* must agree with the form of the noun *book/books* (singular or plural), and English further requires *This book is good* but *These books are good*, where the form of the verb *be* (*is/are*) must agree with the noun phrase *this book* (singular) or *these books* (plural). English has only a small amount of agreement, but many other languages have far more. Compare GOVERNMENT.

alienable possession The property of a POSSESSIVE in which the possessed represents something that could, in principle, be readily separated from the possessor. Examples: *Susie's cigarettes*, *my car*, *their house*. Compare INALIENABLE POSSESSION.

allomorph See under MORPHEME.

alternation Variation in the form of a single MORPHEME, depending on which other morphemes it occurs next to. For example, the morpheme {sane} has the allomorph /seɪn/ in *sane* and *insane*, but the allomorph /sæn/ in *sanity* and *insanity*; the morpheme {electric} has the allomorph /ɪˈlektrɪk/ in *electric* but the allomorph /ɪlekˈtrɪs/ in *electricity*; and the morpheme {leaf} has the allomorph /li:f/ in *leaf* but the allomorph /li:v/ in *leaves*.

ambiguity The presence in a single string of words of two or more sharply distinct meanings. A LEXICAL AMBIGUITY results only from the presence of a word with different meanings, as in *The sailors enjoyed the port*. A STRUCTURAL AMBIGUITY results from assigning different syntactic structures to the words, as in *Visiting relatives can be a nuisance*, *Old men and women are easily frightened*, *The chicken is too hot to eat* and *Anne likes horses more than Mark*. Complex cases are possible, as in *I saw her duck* and the classic *Janet made the robot fast*.

anacoluthon An abrupt change from one syntactic construction to another in the middle of an utterance, leaving the original construction incomplete. Example: *I think you ought to – well, do it your own way*.

analogy The extension of an existing grammatical pattern to new cases. New words entering the language routinely acquire their inflections by analogy with existing words: for example, the new noun *CD-ROM* has acquired its plural *CD-ROMs* by analogy with other nouns like *dog*, plural *dogs*, and the new verb *fax* has acquired its past tense *faxed* by analogy with other verbs like *wash*, past *washed*. But even existing words can change their forms by analogy. For example, the verb *melt* formerly had the participle *molten*, but today this form is confined to use as an ADJECTIVAL PASSIVE, as in *molten metal*, and the participle has otherwise changed to the regular form *melted*, as in *The sun has melted the ice* (not *. . . *molten the ice*), by analogy with other verbs. Analogy need not bring about greater regularity. The verb *catch* formerly had the regular past tense *catched*, but this has been replaced by irregular *caught*, apparently by analogy with *teach*, past *taught*, and some American varieties have altered the past tense of *dive* from *dived* to *dove*, by analogy with verbs like *drive*, past *drove*.

analytic construction Another name for a PERIPHRASTIC construction.

analytic language A language in which the form of each word is invariable, and all grammatical markers are independent words. Vietnamese is a perfect example of such a language, and Chinese and Hawaiian come very close. English is not so strongly analytic, but it does have a significant degree of analytical character. Compare English *I will have loved*, in which every morpheme except the ending *-ed* is an independent word, with its Latin translation *amavero*, in which all the morphemes are bound and the whole thing is a single word.

anaphor (also **pro-form**) An item with little intrinsic meaning or reference of its own which takes its interpretation from another linguistic item in the same sentence or discourse, its ANTECEDENT. In the sentence *I asked Jan to check the proofs, and she did it*, *she* is an anaphor with *Jan* as its antecedent, and *did it* is an anaphor with *check the proofs* as its antecedent. The relation between an anaphor and its antecedent is one of *anaphora*, also called BINDING, COREFERENCE or (rarely) CONSTRUAL: we say that an antecedent binds its anaphor, or that it corefers with it. An anaphor that precedes its antecedent is occasionally called a CATAPHOR; an example is *she* in *After she finished dinner, Susie lit* *a cigarette*. See the entry for ANTECEDENT for further examples, and compare EXOPHOR.

The labels NULL ANAPHOR or ZERO ANAPHOR are sometimes applied to a blank space which functions like an anaphor. In the example *Susie got up and took a shower*, the subject position of the verb *took* is empty (compare . . . *and she took a shower*). This is an example of a null anaphor, since we still understand the empty subject position as referring to *Susie*.

animate A label applied to a NOUN or a NOUN PHRASE which denotes a human being or a higher animal. Examples: *tiger, salesman, student, shark, my mother, the Marx Brothers, that cute little cocker spaniel, the woman you were talking to*. The opposite is INANIMATE.

anomalous Departing in some way from the ordinary rules of the language. When an attempted sentence violates the grammatical rules of the language, we usually describe it as *ungrammatical* or *ill-formed* rather than *anomalous*; see ILL-FORMED. More commonly, we apply the label (*semantically*) *anomalous* to a sentence which is grammatically perfect but impossible to interpret, like the following example, in which the hash mark (#) indicates the anomaly: #*Jezebel killed Ahab, but Ahab didn't die*. Here *Ahab died* is an intrinsic part of the meaning of *killed Ahab*, and so this sentence is incoherent, assuming only one Ahab is involved. Further examples of anomalous sentences are #*The square root of seven is green and squishy* and the celebrated #*Colourless green ideas sleep furiously*, in which words of incompatible meanings are combined.

Note that the following sentence is rather different: *Natalie enjoyed himself at the disco*. Here there is really no linguistic problem at all: it is merely that our experience of the world leads us to expect that a person called *Natalie* will be female. Nor is there any linguistic problem with this next example: *The capital city of the USA is Dallas*. This is not anomalous at all, but merely false.

antecedent 1. A linguistic expression which provides the interpretation for a second expression, an ANAPHOR, which has little intrinsic meaning of its own. Most commonly, an antecedent is a NOUN PHRASE. In the following examples, the first bold italic item is the antecedent and the second is the anaphor referring to it: *If you see* ***Susie****, give* ***her*** *my regards*; ***The children*** *ran to* ***their*** *mother*; ***Jan*** *rang to tell me* ***she'd*** *be* *late;* ***Most of my students*** *have submitted* ***their*** *essays;* ***Susie*** *injured* ***herself*** *playing hockey;* ***Susie and Natalie*** *showed* ***each other*** *their purchases.* Occasionally an antecedent follows its anaphor: *If you see* ***her,*** *give* ***Susie*** *my regards.* It is possible for the antecedent and the anaphor to be in different sentences, and even in utterances produced by two different people: Susie: *I ran into* ***Alice*** *today.* Mike: *How is* ***she*** *getting on in* ***her*** *new job?*

It is possible for an antecedent to belong to another category. Examples: *She asked me to* ***wash the car,*** *and I* ***did it*** (the antecedent is a verb phrase); *This job requires a* ***cordless*** *drill, but I don't have* ***such a*** *thing* (the antecedent is an adjective phrase); *I thought Susie was* ***in the library,*** *but I didn't find her* ***there*** (the antecedent is a prepositional phrase); *I've lost my favourite* ***earrings,*** *and I'll have to get some new* ***ones*** (the antecedent is the word *earrings,* which is only a piece of a noun phrase). The antecedent can even be a complete sentence, as in the following exchange: Susie: *Our budget is being cut.* Mike: *Where did you hear that?* Here the anaphor *that* refers to Susie's entire utterance.

2. See under CONDITIONAL SENTENCE.

aorist A label which has no specific meaning but which is conventionally applied to certain verb-forms in certain languages, most notably in ancient Greek, where the label is conferred upon a set of past-tense forms differing from the PERFECT.

AP The abbreviation for ADJECTIVE PHRASE.

apodosis (also **consequent**) See under CONDITIONAL SENTENCE.

apostrophe The punctuation mark [']. This has four functions.

1. It is used in writing a CONTRACTION to show the place of the omitted letters. Examples: *it's* for *it is* or *it has; she'll* for *she will.*

2. It is used in writing certain words which were formerly contractions, but are no longer regarded as such, such as *o'clock* and *cat-o'-nine-tails.*

3. It is used in writing most POSSESSIVES, as in *Jan's brother, children's shoes, my parents' wedding* and *two weeks' work.* But it is *not* used in writing the possessive forms of most PRONOUNS: *The bull lowered its head; Whose umbrella is this?; These books are hers.*

4. Though it is not normally used in writing PLURALS (see GREEN-

GROCER'S APOSTROPHE), it is used in writing the plurals of letters and other forms which would otherwise be difficult to read: *Mind your p's and q's*.

For more on its use, see chapter 5 of *The Penguin Guide to Punctuation*.

appellative An old-fashioned term for COMMON NOUN.

appositive A NOUN PHRASE which immediately follows another noun phrase of identical reference. Appositives are typically NON-RESTRICTIVE: the reference of the first noun phrase is clear, and the appositive serves only to add further information. In writing, an appositive of this sort must be set off by commas. The phrases set off by commas in the following examples are appositives of this sort: *Mexico City*[, *the largest city in the Americas,*] *suffers from fearful pollution*; *His newest book*[, *the last one in the trilogy,*] *concludes the saga*. In each case, removal of the appositive would leave a sentence which is both grammatical and sensible. But an appositive can also be RESTRICTIVE (required for identification of the reference of the first noun phrase). Such an appositive is not set off by commas in writing. An example is *Shelley* in the sentence *I'm writing a biography of the poet Shelley*. Here, removing *Shelley* would leave a result which is impossible to interpret: we would have no idea which poet was being referred to.

An appositive is said to be in apposition with the preceding phrase.

appositive clause Another name for a NON-RESTRICTIVE RELATIVE CLAUSE; see under RELATIVE CLAUSE.

arbitrary control See under CONTROL.

archaism A word or a form which was normal long ago but which has generally disappeared from the language and is used occasionally only for special effect. Examples include the *hath* of *What hath God wrought?* (Marconi's first trans-Atlantic radio message) and the *wilt, thou* and *thy* of *Wilt thou take this woman to be thy lawfully wedded wife?* (in one version of the marriage service).

argument A NOUN PHRASE whose presence in a sentence is absolutely required by the verb of that sentence. For example, in the sentence *The Mongols destroyed Kiev*, both *The Mongols* and *Kiev* are arguments, since the verb *destroy* requires these two slots to be filled, and leaving either empty would produce ungrammaticality. In contrast, all further phrases that might be added are optional, and not required to produce a grammatical result: *in the year 1240*, *out of revenge*, *angrily*, *at the command of the Great Khan*, and so on. These optional elements are ADJUNCTS. See VALENCY.

article A DETERMINER which has little meaning of its own but serves to indicate that the NOUN PHRASE containing it is definite or indefinite, specific or non-specific. English has two articles, the DEFINITE ARTICLE *the* and the INDEFINITE ARTICLE *a*(*n*). The definite article typically indicates that what its noun phrase denotes is either already known to the listener or easily guessable from the context: for example, *the girl* can usually only be used if the girl in question has already been identified earlier, while *the waiter* can be used if the scene has already been set in a restaurant, where the presence of a waiter would naturally be assumed. The indefinite article is used when its noun phrase does not meet these conditions: if we want to introduce a bus into the conversation for the first time, we must normally say *a bus*, unless the context has already made it clear that the presence of a bus is not surprising, as in *I had finished my shopping and was ready to go home, so I got on the bus*.

The English indefinite article does not distinguish between specific and non-specific interpretations. For example, *I'm looking for a cookery book* can equally mean 'I'm looking for a specific cookery book' or 'I'm looking for any old cookery book'.

ascriptive sentence A sentence in which a (temporary or permanent) quality is ascribed to somebody or something. In English, an ascriptive sentence is usually constructed with the COPULA *be*: *Susie is pretty*; *Susie is clever*; *Susie is Irish*; *Susie is drunk*. But sometimes we use *have* instead: *Susie has blue eyes*; *Susie has a temper*. In each case, some property (prettiness, inebriation, blue eyes, or whatever) is being attributed to Susie. Unlike an EQUATIONAL SENTENCE, an ascriptive sentence cannot be turned round: **Pretty is Susie*; **Drunk is Susie*.

aspect The GRAMMATICAL CATEGORY which indicates how the time-structure of the activity or state described by a sentence is viewed: as a structureless whole, as continuing over time, as a series of repetitions, as a habit, as beginning or ending, and so on. Aspect must be carefully distinguished from TENSE – grammatical *location* in time – even though the formal expressions of these two categories are often deeply intermingled in particular languages.

For example, the English sentences *I drank brandy*, *I was drinking brandy* and *I used to drink brandy* are all identical in tense – they are all in the past tense – but they differ in aspect: the first presents my brandy-drinking as an unanalysed whole, the second presents it as a continuing action, and the third presents it as a habitual activity.

Aspectual distinctions are mostly classified into two superordinate types: PERFECTIVE (no internal structure) and IMPERFECTIVE (some kind of internal structure), with the second subdivided into several more specific types. The English PERFECT is also often classed as an aspect, even though it is rather unusual among aspects. See these terms for more information.

aspectual verb A VERB which does not itself denote any particular action, event or state, but which serves to indicate that the action or state denoted by another verb or an adjective is beginning, continuing, ending or changing. Among our aspectual verbs are *start, begin, continue, keep* (*on*), *stop, quit, finish, become, get* (when this means 'become') and *turn*. Examples: *Susie started eating*; *Susie kept* (*on*) *driving*; *Susie quit smoking*; *Susie got angry*; *Susie turned ugly*.

asterisk The symbol *, conventionally placed in front of a string of linguistic material to show that it is ill-formed (ungrammatical), as in **She smiled me*.

asyndeton The joining together of two or more complete sentences without the use of a coordinating CONJUNCTION. Examples: *I came, I saw, I conquered*; *It was the best of times; it was the worst of times*; *The biologists have fossils; we linguists don't*. Such a construction is said to be asyndetic.

atelic A label applied to a verb or a sentence which denotes an activity or state which has no recognizable goal whose achievement would necessarily bring the activity or state to an end. Atelic verbs include *sleep* (as in *Susie is sleeping*), *speak* (as in *Susie speaks good French*) and *remember* (as in *I remember the summer of 1970*). The opposite is TELIC.

attraction The grammatical phenomenon in which a verb shows AGREEMENT, not with its logical subject, but with something else, typically something which is closer to it. An example is *I wonder if the right kind of supplies are being sent*, in which the plural verb-form *are* is agreeing, not with its logical (and singular) subject *kind*, but with the nearby plural noun *supplies*. Occasionally attraction occurs in the other direction: in the example *She is one of those people who is always critical of everybody else*, the verb should logically be *are*, since its subject is *people*, but *is* has been used to agree with *one*, which is further away.

attributive Inside a NOUN PHRASE, the position between the DETERMINER (if any) and the HEAD noun. In the following example, the blank indicates the attributive position: *a* __ *textbook*. In English, the attributive position may be filled either by an ADJECTIVE, like *new*, or by a NOUN, like *linguistics*. Compare PREDICATIVE.

auxiliary (in traditional grammar, **helping verb**) In English, one of a small set of items which have certain properties in common with verbs but which also exhibit some distinctive characteristics of their own. Most linguists regard the English auxiliaries as a subclass of VERBS, but a minority view sees them as forming an entirely distinct PART OF SPEECH.

Our auxiliaries are divided into two types: the PRIMARY AUXILIARIES *be* and *have*, plus the 'dummy' auxiliary *do*, and the MODAL AUXILIARIES *can, could, will, would, shall, should, may, might, must* and *ought* (*to*). The two SEMI-AUXILIARIES *need* and *dare* are anomalous, behaving sometimes like modals but at other times like LEXICAL VERBS (ordinary verbs); see this entry.

The auxiliaries share the following properties with lexical verbs:

1. They occupy the same position in the sentence, typically immediately after the SUBJECT: *Jessica bought a teddy-bear; Jessica should go home.*

2. They exhibit SEQUENCE OF TENSES: *Jessica says she drinks vodka; Jessica said she drank vodka; Jessica says she will come; Jessica said she would come.*

3. The primary auxiliaries (but not the modal auxiliaries) take the present-tense third-singular ending *-s* and form PARTICIPLES: *Jessica wants a drink; Jessica has finished her drink*; but not **Jessica cans speak French*; *Finishing her drink, Jessica stood up; Having finished her drink, Jessica stood up*; but not **woulding* or **oughting*.

The auxiliaries differ from lexical verbs in four respects:

1. Only auxiliaries allow NEGATION: *Jessica isn't smoking*; *Jessica shouldn't smoke*; but **Jessica smokes not / smokesn't*.

2. Only auxiliaries can undergo INVERSION with the subject: *Is Jessica smoking?*; *Should Jessica smoke?*; but **Smokes Jessica?*.

3. Only auxiliaries can appear in TAG QUESTIONS, a property sometimes called 'code': *Jessica smokes, doesn't she?*; *Jessica isn't smoking, is she?*; but **Jessica doesn't smoke, smokes she?*.

4. Only auxiliaries can receive EMPHATIC STRESS to contradict a preceding statement: if you say *Jessica isn't smoking* or *Jessica doesn't smoke*, I can contradict you with *Jessica IS smoking* or *Jessica DOES smoke*, but not with **Jessica SMOKES*.

These four properties are sometimes called the NICE PROPERTIES as a mnemonic. The 'dummy' auxiliary *do* is used whenever one of these four properties must be added to a sentence which contains no other auxiliary: *Jessica smokes*; *Jessica doesn't smoke*; *Does Jessica smoke?*; *Jessica smokes, doesn't she?*; *Jessica DOES smoke*.

B

back-formation A particular type of WORD-FORMATION, or a word formed in this way. In back-formation, we take an existing word and remove from it a piece that *looks* like an affix, but really isn't, in order to obtain a new word. For example, the words *burglar*, *sculptor* and *editor*, which are borrowed from Old French or from Latin, all *sound* as though they contain the familiar agent suffix *-er*, as in *writer* and *singer*, and so we have removed this apparent suffix to obtain the previously non-existence verbs *burgle*, *sculpt* and *edit*. Other examples of back-formation are *pea* from earlier *pease* (which sounds like a plural, but originally wasn't) and *televise* from *television*.

backshift Another term for SEQUENCE OF TENSES.

bahuvrihi (also **headless compound**, **exocentric compound**) A type of COMPOUND in which neither element is a HEAD. For example, a *hatchback* is not a type of back, nor is it a type of hatch: it is a type of car. Other bahuvrihis are *redhead*, *hard-hat* and *highbrow* (all types of person) and *pickpocket*. Compare ENDOCENTRIC COMPOUND.

bare infinitive An infinitive not preceded by *to*. See under INFINITIVE.

bare-NP adverbial An ADVERBIAL which consists of a NOUN PHRASE with no preposition. Examples (in brackets): *Do it* [*this way*]; *Get started* [*the minute she arrives*]; *I've seen that* [*every place I've been*].

base In WORD-FORMATION, the form which is the direct source of another form. For example, *happy* is the base for forming all of *happily*, *unhappy* and *happiness*, while *unhappy* is the base for forming both *unhappily* and *unhappiness*.

basic word order In any given language, the order in which the major units of a sentence most commonly appear. Basic word order is commonly formulated in terms of the SUBJECT (S), the OBJECT (O) and the VERB (V). In English, the basic word order is SVO: *Susie kissed Natalie*. Other orders are unusual (*Natalie Susie kissed*) or impossible (**Kissed Natalie Susie*). But other languages are different: Japanese, Turkish and Basque are SOV; Welsh, Irish and Classical Arabic are VSO; Malagasy (in Madagascar) is VOS; and so on.

benefactive (also **beneficiary**) The SEMANTIC ROLE assigned to a NOUN PHRASE denoting a person who benefits from some action. In the following examples, *Susie* is a beneficiary: *I've knitted Susie a sweater*; *Mike has fixed the washing machine for Susie*. In some CASE languages, there is a specific *benefactive* case-form for expressing this.

binding Another term for anaphora; see under ANAPHOR.

blending A kind of WORD-FORMATION in which a word is constructed by combining arbitrary parts of two or more existing words. Examples include *smog* (*smoke* plus *fog*), *brunch* (*breakfast* plus *lunch*) and *rockumentary* (*rock* plus *documentary*). Occasionally all parts of both words are retained, as in *sexploitation* (*sex* plus *exploitation*) and *guesstimate* (*guess* plus *estimate*). A word constructed in such a way is a blend.

blocking The phenomenon in which a perfectly regularly formed word is prevented from existing by the existence of another word of identical meaning. For example, an English verb can usually take the suffix *-er* to denote the agent of that verb: *singer* from *sing*, *writer* from *write*, *smoker* from *smoke*, and so on. But *steal* does not yield **stealer*, because this is blocked by *thief*, and, while *curious* yields *curiosity*, *furious* does not yield **furiosity*, because this is blocked by *fury*.

block language The distinctive type of language used in public signs, typically consisting of PHRASES, rather than of complete SENTENCES. Examples: *No Parking*; *Left turn only*; *Stage door*; *EU passports*; *Birmingham and the North*; *Open Sundays*. Compare HEADLINE LANGUAGE.

bold face Dark type, **like this**. Boldface is used for highlighting, most obviously for headwords in dictionaries, as in this one.

borrowing Copying a word from one language into another language. English has borrowed vast numbers of words from other languages: *lettuce* from Latin, *virgin* from Norman French, *pretzel* from German, *cigarette* from modern French, *sherry* from Spanish, *ski* from Norwegian, *ombudsman* from Swedish, *retsina* from modern Greek, *tea* from Chinese, *algebra* from Arabic, *yogurt* from Turkish, *ukulele* from Hawaiian, *sushi* from Japanese, *pyjamas* from Hindi, *kangaroo* from the Guugu-Yimidhirr language of Australia, and countless others. Indeed, the modern English vocabulary is about seventy per cent borrowed, with Norman French, Latin and ancient Greek being the main donor languages. A borrowed word is called a LOANWORD.

bound morpheme A MORPHEME which cannot stand alone to make a word, but which must be combined with at least one other morpheme within a word. The most familiar type of bound morpheme is an AFFIX (a prefix or a suffix). Most affixes in English are grammatical in nature, like the prefixes *un-* (as in *uninteresting*) and *re-* (as in *rewrite*) and the suffixes *-ly* (as in *slowly*) and *-ness* (as in *happiness*). A few, though, are not really grammatical, like the *step-* of *stepmother* (which has nothing to do with the independent word *step*) and the *anti-* of *anti-war*. But our technical terms are largely constructed from another type of bound morpheme, the COMBINING FORMS (sense 2); see that entry.

bracketing A way of displaying the syntactic structure of a phrase or a sentence. Each syntactic unit which is recognized is enclosed within a pair of square brackets. For example, the phrase *the little girl* would be bracketed as follows: [[*the*] [[*little*] [*girl*]]]. This shows that the phrase consists of *little* plus *girl*, which form a unit *little girl*, which in turn combines with *the* to form the complete phrase. If the bracketed units are labelled to show what SYNTACTIC CATEGORY they belong to, the result is a labelled bracketing: $[_{\mathrm{NP}}[_{\mathrm{Det}}\textit{the}]\ [_{\mathrm{N'}}[_{\mathrm{A}}\textit{little}]\ [_{\mathrm{N}}\textit{girl}]]]$. This shows that *little* is an adjective, that *girl* is a noun, that *little girl* is of the category that linguists call an N-bar, that *the* is a determiner, and that the whole thing is a noun phrase.

C

calque (also **loan-translation**) A word which is constructed by translating a word in another language piece by piece, or the process of forming a word in such a way. For example, Greek *sympathia* 'sympathy, compassion', which consists of *syn-* 'with' plus *pathia* 'feeling', was calqued into Latin as *compassio*, from *con-* 'with' and *passio* 'feeling'. English rarely forms calques, but one example is *it goes without saying*, calqued on French *il va sans dire*.

canonical A label applied to any pattern in a language which represents the most typical or usual pattern in some domain. For example, the canonical pattern for forming plurals in English is with *-s*, as in *books*, *islands* and *CD-ROMs*, even though there are exceptional plurals like *sheep*, *women*, *teeth* and *phenomena*.

cardinal numeral A counting number: any one of the linguistic items of the type *one*, *two*, *three*, *twelve*, *twenty-seven*, and so on. The English cardinal numerals exhibit some rather distinctive grammatical properties, and it is not easy to assign them to a PART OF SPEECH. Some linguists class them as DETERMINERS, others as ADJECTIVES, and still others as a separate category of their own. Compare ORDINAL NUMERAL.

case In some languages, an ending (or other modification) attached to a NOUN or to a NOUN PHRASE to express its relation to the rest of the sentence. In English, case is exhibited only by a few PRONOUNS: we say *I saw her* but *She saw me*, where *I* and *me*, and also *she* and *her*, are two different case-forms of the same pronoun.

Some other languages have far more in the way of case. Basque, for example, has about a dozen cases, and these are attached to all noun phrases. With *neska* 'the girl', for example, we have sentences like *Neska ikusi dut* 'I saw the girl', *Neskak ikusi nau* 'The girl saw me', *Neskari eman diot* 'I gave it to the girl', *Neskarekin joan naiz* 'I went with the girl', *Neskaren lagunak hemen daude* 'The girl's friends are here', and a number of others.

case grammar Any approach to grammatical description which stresses the importance of SEMANTIC ROLES. Case grammar was developed in the 1960s and is still favoured in some quarters today, though most practical grammars of English pay little attention to it.

catachresis A formal or old-fashioned term for MALAPROPISM.

cataphor See under ANAPHOR.

catenative verb A VERB which is commonly followed by another verb, often with the infinitival *to* intervening. Examples include *want* in *I want to go home, need* in *We need to draw up a budget, quit* in *Susie quit smoking,* and *start* in *She started to run.* Different linguists define the term somewhat differently, but note that a verb followed by a verb of purpose, such as *babysit* in *She babysat to earn extra money,* is not normally regarded as a catenative verb by anybody.

causative A construction meaning that somebody caused somebody else to do something. Given the simple sentence *I washed the car,* the most usual causative pattern in English is illustrated by *She made me wash the car,* though other patterns are possible, such as *She got me to wash the car,* and, in American English, *She had me wash the car.* Some (but not all) linguists would extend this label to cases like *I had my car repaired,* whose source is roughly *Somebody repaired my car.*

circumstantial clause Any ADVERBIAL CLAUSE expressing circumstance, such as the bracketed clause in [*Since the weather looks threatening,*] *let's forget about our picnic.*

citation form That form of a word which is conventionally used in naming it, talking about it or entering it in a dictionary, such as *dog, big* or *take.*

clause A grammatical unit consisting of a SUBJECT and a PREDICATE. There are two principal types of clause: a MAIN CLAUSE can possibly stand alone to make a sentence by itself, while a SUBORDINATE CLAUSE must be attached to another clause within a larger sentence. Every SENTENCE must contain at least one main clause, though a sentence may contain two or more main clauses, and in any case may additionally contain one or more subordinate clauses. For example, the sentence *Mike started making dinner* consists of a single main clause, while the sentence *Mike started making dinner and Susie tidied the lounge* consists of two main clauses connected by *and*, and the sentence *Mike started making dinner while Susie tidied the lounge* consists of a main clause plus a subordinate clause beginning with *while*.

A SIMPLE SENTENCE consists of a single main clause. A COMPOUND SENTENCE consists of two or more main clauses. A COMPLEX SENTENCE consists of one main clause plus one or more subordinate clauses. A COMPOUND-COMPLEX SENTENCE consists of two or more main clauses plus one or more subordinate clauses. See these entries for examples.

In traditional grammar, and still today for most linguists, a clause must contain a verb which is FINITE (marked for TENSE). In this view, the bracketed sequences in the following example would not be clauses, but only PHRASES within a single large clause: [*Having finished her dinner,*] *Susie settled down* [*to study*] [*in order to prepare for her exams*]. In some current theories of grammar, however, every verb must be assigned to its own clause, and hence all of the bracketed sequences would count as clauses.

cleft Any of various constructions in which some element of a sentence is removed from its normal position and certain extra words are added to highlight the cleft. The purpose of a cleft is to place the clefted element into FOCUS. For example, starting with the sentence *Mike wants a new car,* we can form an IT-CLEFT to focus either on *Mike* (*It's Mike who wants a new car*) or on *a new car* (*It's a new car that Mike wants*). Or we can form a WH-CLEFT (or PSEUDO-CLEFT) to focus on *a new car*: *What Mike wants is a new car* or *A new car is what Mike wants*.

clipping A type of WORD-FORMATION in which a short piece is extracted from a longer word and given the same meaning. Examples include *bra* from *brassière, gym* from *gymnasium, flu* from *influenza, cello* from *violoncello, phone* from *telephone* and *bus* from *omnibus*. A word formed in this way is a clipped form. A clipped form is a real word, and not an ABBREVIATION. A clipped form may continue to co-exist with its source word, like *gym* and *flu*, or it may largely or wholly displace its source word, like *bra* and *bus*.

clitic An element of a sentence which is less than an independent word but more than an AFFIX. A clitic is usually quite short, and it is fixed into a certain position from which it may not be moved. English is not rich in clitics, but the *'ll* of *I'll be right there* is perhaps best viewed as a clitic attached to the preceding *I*. French has many more clitics: for example, in *Il te le donnera* 'He'll give it to you', the pronouns *il* 'he', *te* 'you' and *le* 'it' are all clitics: they must occur directly before the verb *donnera* 'will give' and only in the order given. The material to which a clitic is attached is its host. For example, *I* is the host for *'ll* in *I'll*, and *donnera* is the host for the French clitics. A clitic which precedes its host, like the French ones, is a PROCLITIC, while a clitic which follows its host, like English *'ll*, is an ENCLITIC.

closed class A PART OF SPEECH which is small and which rarely accepts new members. English examples include PREPOSITION, DETERMINER and PRONOUN. The opposite is an OPEN CLASS.

cognate object A DIRECT OBJECT which merely repeats the meaning of its verb, such as *dream* in *I dreamt a wonderful dream last night* and *thoughts* in *I'm thinking terrible thoughts*.

coherence The property of a TEXT which hangs together in a readily intelligible manner, which 'makes sense'. For example, in response to the question *Is Susie coming to Mike's party?*, a coherent answer might be any of *Yes*, *I don't know*, *Susie is not speaking to Mike's girlfriend* or *Is the sun going to rise tomorrow?* But a response like *The specific gravity of mercury is 13.6* is unlikely to be coherent. Compare COHESION.

cohesion The use of linguistic devices to connect the elements of a TEXT. For example, in response to the question *Is Susie coming to Mike's party?*, the reply *She's looking forward to it* exhibits cohesion, in that *she* refers to *Susie* and *it* refers to *Mike's party*. Compare COHERENCE.

collective noun A NOUN which denotes a collection of individual persons or objects, such as *committee*, *team*, *government* and *herd*. In some varieties of English, including British English, a collective noun may be treated either as singular (if the whole group is being thought of as a unit) or as plural (if the group is being regarded as a collection of individuals): hence we may say *The committee has announced its decision* (the committee is regarded as a unit) or *The committee are divided on this issue* (the committee is regarded as a group of individuals). In other varieties, especially in American English, a collective noun is always treated as singular, and Americans say *The committee is divided on this issue*. Names of sports teams are treated differently in British and American English: a Briton says *Liverpool are playing Arsenal*, while an American says *Buffalo is playing Dallas*.

colloquialism A word or phrase which is typical of COLLOQUIAL SPEECH but not of formal speech or writing, such as *bummer* or *Get a life!*

colloquial speech Informal everyday speech, of the sort that everybody uses in relaxed circumstances. Colloquial speech is normal for all of us. It is not, in general, ignorant, vulgar or wrong; it is merely different from the sort of language we use in formal speech or writing, when we are being self-conscious and careful. A speaker who never used colloquial speech at all, but who used only formal English in all contexts, would be abnormal.

colon The punctuation mark [:]. This is almost always used after a complete sentence, and its function is to indicate that what follows is an explanation or elaboration of what precedes. Examples: *I propose the creation of a new post: School Executive Officer; I've found the problem: a faulty heating element.* A colon is never preceded by a white space, and it is never followed by a dash or a hyphen. For more on its use, see chapter 4 of *The Penguin Guide to Punctuation*.

combining form **1**. A special form taken by a word when it forms part of a larger word. For example, *piano* takes the combining form *pian-* in *pianist*. Native English words do not usually have distinctive combining forms.

2. An element, usually one taken from Latin or Greek, which never stands alone, but can only appear as part of a larger word. For example, *bibliophile* 'lover of books' consists of the combining forms *biblio-* 'book' and *-phile* 'lover'; neither of these can stand alone, but both recur in other formations, such as *bibliography* 'list of books' and *thermophile* 'heat-lover'. Most English technical terms are constructed from combining forms of this sort.

comitative The relation 'in the company of', usually expressed in English by the preposition *with*, as in *Susie went to the party with Dave*. Some CASE languages have a special case-form for this purpose.

comma The punctuation mark [,]. This has four uses.

1. A *listing comma* is used to connect the items in a list, except for the last two, which are connected by a CONJUNCTION like *and* or *or*. Example: *The Three Musketeers were Athos, Porthos and Aramis*.

2. A *joining comma* is used to join two complete sentences into a single sentence, and it must be followed by a connecting word like *and*, *or*, *but*, *while* or *yet* (but not *however*, which requires a SEMICOLON). Example: *A dropped goal counts three points in rugby union, while in rugby league it counts only one point.*

3. A *gapping comma* is used to show that certain words have been omitted instead of repeated. Example: *Larry decided to order the chicken pathia and Jan, the duck special*. (The omitted words are *decided to order*.)

4. A *pair* of *bracketing commas* is used to set off a weak interruption to a sentence, one which does not greatly interrupt its flow. Example: *She groped for her cigarettes and, finding them, hastily lit one*. (The weak interruption *finding them* could in principle be omitted without destroying the sentence.)

For more on the use of the comma, see chapter 3 of *The Penguin Guide to Punctuation*.

command The (functional) SENTENCE TYPE of any utterance used to issue instructions. This may be done by using an IMPERATIVE sentence: *Wash your hands!*; *Sit down!* But it can also be done by using other sentence types: *You must go home now* (with the DECLARATIVE form more typical of a STATEMENT); *Will you shut up?* (with the INTERROGATIVE form more typical of a QUESTION).

comment In some analyses of sentence structure, that part of a sentence which expresses new information, as opposed to the TOPIC, which expresses old information. For example, in reply to the question *What does Susie do?*, the reply *She's a publisher* consists of the topic *she* and the comment *is a publisher*. Not every sentence has a topic/comment structure.

common gender In a language with GENDER, the property of a noun which can be assigned to more than one gender, depending on what it refers to. For example, the French nouns *enfant* 'child' and *hypocrite* 'hypocrite' are masculine when referring to males but feminine when referring to females. Occasionally, though rather unnecessarily, the label is extended to English nouns which can denote people of either sex, like *teacher* and *doctor*, as opposed to those which mark sex, like *host/hostess* and *widow/widower*. Compare EPICENE.

common noun (formerly also **appellative**) An ordinary NOUN, one which denotes a class of things, such as *dog, pencil, explosion* or *happiness*. Compare PROPER NOUN.

comparative That form of an ADJECTIVE or an ADVERB which is constructed either with *-er* or with *more* and which serves to express a higher degree of the quality denoted by the base word. Examples are *bigger* from *big, worse* from *bad, more beautiful* from *beautiful* and *more carefully* from *carefully*. English also has a comparative of inferiority, constructed with *less*, as in *less interesting*. See DEGREE and ABSOLUTE COMPARATIVE, and compare POSITIVE, SUPERLATIVE.

comparative clause A CLAUSE attached to a COMPARATIVE. Examples, with the comparative clauses bracketed: *My ticket was more expensive* [*than I expected*]; *Mike is taller* [*than I am*]; *His latest film has been less successful* [*than his other films have been*]. When no VERB is present, the comparative expression is only a PHRASE, not a clause: *Mike is taller* [*than me*]; *His last film has been less successful* [*than his other films*]. Quite often, an EQUATIVE clause is classed as a comparative clause: *Susie drives as well* [*as I do*].

competence The abstract knowledge of your language which you have in your head; the knowledge which allows you to speak and to understand your language easily. Compare PERFORMANCE.

complement A label which is applied variously to several quite different things.

1. A subject complement is a phrase which follows a COPULA or a QUASI-COPULA and either modifies the subject or denotes something identical to the subject. Examples (in brackets): *Jan is* [*a senior administrator*]; *Susie became* [*a journalist*]; *The children were* [*very excited*]; *Susie is* [*in the shower*].

2. An object complement is a phrase which follows a DIRECT OBJECT and either modifies that object or denotes something identical to it. Examples (in brackets): *I consider hang-gliding* [*dangerous*]; Stage Coach *made John Wayne* [*a star*].

3. The complement of a lexical HEAD is a phrase which directly follows it and, in some broad sense, 'completes' it. Examples (in brackets): *Susie is fond* [*of chocolate*] (*of chocolate* is the complement of the adjective *fond*); *I am sorry* [*to tell you this*] (*to tell you this* is the complement of the adjective *sorry*); *Let's get a bottle* [*of wine*] (*of wine* is the complement of the noun *bottle*); *The cat is under* [*the bed*] (*the bed* is the complement of the preposition *under*; this is the same as the OBJECT of the preposition); *Susie has bought* [*a new car*] (*a new car* is the complement of the verb *bought*; this is the same as the DIRECT OBJECT of the verb); *She wants* [*to find a new job*] (*to find a new job* is the complement of the verb *wants*). The use of *complement* for *object* is now rather old-fashioned.

4. In some older approaches to grammar, the label *complement* is applied to every phrase following a VERB. In this approach, the sentence *I saw Lisa in town yesterday* contains three complements to the verb *saw*: *Lisa*, *in town* and *yesterday*.

5. In some recent theories of grammar, the label *complement* (of a verb) is applied to the entire VERB PHRASE containing that verb except for the verb itself. In this approach, the verb phrase *saw Lisa in town yesterday* consists of the verb *saw* and the complement *Lisa in town yesterday*. This usage is not normal in most circles.

6. Short for COMPLEMENT CLAUSE.

complement clause (also **complement**, for short) A CLAUSE which is introduced by a COMPLEMENTIZER (though this may sometimes be optionally omitted) and which is attached to a preceding noun, adjective or verb. In *The report that mobile phones cause memory loss has been challenged*, *that mobile phones cause memory loss* is a NOUN-COMPLEMENT CLAUSE attached to the noun *report*. In *I am sure that Susie is coming*, *that Susie is coming* is an adjective-complement clause attached to the adjective *sure*. In *My doctor says that I drink too much*, *that I drink too much* is a VERB-COMPLEMENT CLAUSE attached to the verb *says*. In the second and third of these, but not in the first, the complementizer *that* may be optionally omitted.

Note that a noun-complement clause is different from a RELATIVE CLAUSE, even though the two are often superficially similar. In *The reports that Ted is sending poison-pen letters are surprising, that Ted is sending poison-pen letters* is a noun-complement clause attached to the noun *reports*. But in *The reports that Ted is sending are surprising, that Ted is sending* is a relative clause attached to *reports*.

Note: traditionally, and still today for most linguists, a complement clause, like any clause, must be FINITE (marked for TENSE). Hence, in *Susie wants to see that new film*, the complement *to see that new film* is only a PHRASE, and not a clause. However, in some current theories of grammar, every verb must be assigned to its own clause, and so this complement would be regarded as a complement clause.

See also SENTENTIAL SUBJECT.

complementizer The PART OF SPEECH which includes the words which introduce COMPLEMENT CLAUSES, most commonly *that* and *whether* (and also *if*, when this means *whether*). Examples of use: *She said that she was coming; I don't know whether she's coming.*

complex preposition A PREPOSITION which consists of two or three words, such as *in spite of, in front of, out of* and *on top of.* In spite of their form, such items behave like simple prepositions.

complex sentence A sentence which contains at least one SUBORDINATE CLAUSE. In the following examples, the subordinate clauses are bracketed: *Susie said* [*that she would come*]; [*After Susie got up,*] *she took a shower; The scientists* [*who believe* [*that there may be life on Mars*]] *suspect* [*that it exists below the surface*]. Compare COMPOUND SENTENCE.

composition A slightly old-fashioned word for the formation of a COMPOUND.

compound A word constructed by combining two or more existing words. The meaning of a compound is not always predictable from the meanings of its component parts: for example, not every board which is black is a *blackboard*, and not every friend who is a girl is your *girlfriend*. The formation of a compound is compounding.

compound sentence A sentence which contains two or more MAIN CLAUSES but no SUBORDINATE CLAUSES. The clauses in a compound sentence are often connected by a CONJUNCTION like *and*, *or* or *yet*. In the following examples, the main clauses are bracketed: [*Susie smokes*] *but* [*Mike doesn't*]; [*The Turks captured Constantinople in 1453,*] *and* [*that was the end of the Byzantine Empire*]; [*It was the best of times;*] [*it was the worst of times*]; [*Susie wants a brandy,*] [*Mike wants a whisky,*] *and* [*Natalie would like a Cointreau.*] Compare COMPLEX SENTENCE.

compound-complex sentence A sentence which is both a COMPOUND SENTENCE and a COMPLEX SENTENCE: that is, it contains at least two MAIN CLAUSES and at least one SUBORDINATE CLAUSE. Example: *After she left university, Susie moved to London and her boyfriend followed her*.

concessive clause An ADVERBIAL CLAUSE which expresses the sense of *although*. Examples include the first clauses in *Although it had been raining for days, the cricket pitch was in perfect condition* and *Even though Susie speaks fluent Italian, she could not understand the Genoese dialect*.

concord Another term for AGREEMENT.

concrete noun A NOUN which denotes something which is physical and can be touched, such as *dog*, *plastic*, *grass* and *brother*. Compare ABSTRACT NOUN.

conditional In English, a traditional label for the MODAL AUXILIARY *would*, and also for *should*, when this does not express obligation. The name is given because sentences with these auxiliaries often seem to imply an unstated condition. For example, the sentence *I would like a drink* appears to imply something like 'if I had a choice', even though, in practice, this is merely a polite way of asking for a drink. This label is now considered somewhat old-fashioned. But certain other languages, such as French, do have a distinctive set of verb-forms called the *conditional*.

conditional sentence Any sentence of the form *if . . .* (*then*). There are two types. In an open conditional, the fulfilment of the condition is seen as a realistic possibility. Examples: *If Susie gets a promotion, she plans to buy a new car; You'll have to go outside if you want to smoke*. In a COUNTERFACTUAL, the condition is seen as contrary to fact. Examples: *If I spoke better French, I could get a job in Paris; If McClelland had been more aggressive, the American Civil War might have ended two years earlier*. In both cases, the clause with *if* is called the PROTASIS or ANTECEDENT, while the other clause is the APODOSIS or CONSEQUENT.

conjoined See under COORDINATE STRUCTURE.

conjugation **1**. Changing the form of a VERB for grammatical purposes. For example, the English verb *take* may appear as any of *take, takes, took, taken* or *taking*, depending upon its grammatical position.

2. In some languages (not including English), a class of verbs whose members change their forms in the same way for grammatical purposes. For example, Spanish has three conjugations: the *-ar* verbs, the *-er* verbs and the *-ir* verbs. Once you have learned how to make the forms of a single *-ar* verb, such as *amar* 'love', you can immediately make the forms of all other *-ar* verbs (apart from any which may be irregular), but you still have to learn the other two classes separately.

conjunct **1**. Any one of the items linked by a word like *and* with a COORDINATE STRUCTURE. Examples (in brackets): [*Susie*] *and* [*her parents*] are coming to dinner.

2. In the QUIRK GRAMMARS, a label applied to an ADVERBIAL which connects its sentence to neighbouring sentences, such as *moreover, nevertheless, finally* or *in addition*.

conjunction **1**. The PART OF SPEECH which can combine two or more linguistic items in a COORDINATE STRUCTURE, such as *and, or* and *but*. Examples: *Susie smokes and drinks; She is clever but careless; Would you prefer to stir-fry the vegetables or to make the salad?*

2. Another term for coordinate structure.

consequent See under CONDITIONAL SENTENCE.

constituent Any sequence of one or more words which functions as a grammatical unit within a sentence. See CONSTITUENT STRUCTURE.

constituent structure (also **phrase structure**) The type of structure typically exhibited by a sentence in English and in most other languages. Constituent structure is *hierarchical* in nature. The sentence consists of two or three smaller units, each of which consists of some still smaller units, each of which consists of some even smaller units, and so on, until we reach the smallest units, which we may take either as WORDS or as MORPHEMES.

Consider the sentence *The little girl hugged her dolly*. This consists of two large constituents, its IMMEDIATE CONSTITUENTS: *the little girl* and *hugged her dolly*. The first consists of two smaller constituents (its immediate constituents): *the* and *little girl*, with the second in turn consisting of *little* and *girl*. The second original constituent consists of *hugged* and *her dolly*, with the latter consisting of *her* plus *dolly*. The constituent structure of the whole sentence can be displayed by means of a BRACKETING: [[[*the*] [[*little*] [*girl*]]] [[*hugged*] [[*her*] [*dolly*]]]].

construal **1**. Another term for PARSING, now somewhat old-fashioned. We may say, for example, that in *She took off her jumper* the word *off* is construed with (forms a unit with) *took*, while in *She jumped off the pier* the word *off* is construed with *the pier*.

2. Another term for anaphora; see under ANAPHOR.

construction Any grammatical structure which occurs systematically in a language, or a particular instance of it. English examples include the CONTINUOUS, the PERFECT, TOPICALIZATION and PREPOSITION STRANDING.

contamination The process in which the form of a word is altered in a somewhat arbitrary way because of the influence of another word of similar form or meaning. An example is the alteration of *regardless*, in non-standard English, to *irregardless*, by contamination from *irrespectively*.

continuous (also **progressive**) A particular ASPECT form, a variety of the IMPERFECTIVE, which indicates that the action of the verb is, was or will be in progress or continuing over a period of time. In English, the continuous is expressed with the *be -ing* construction. Examples: *Susie is eating dinner; Susie was taking a shower when the phone rang; Susie will be vacationing in Hawaii this summer; Susie's car is being serviced; Susie is smoking a lot these days.*

contraction A short way of pronouncing, and writing, a series of two or more words. Examples include *can't* for *can not, she'll* for *she will*, and *we'd've* for *we would have.*

control The process by which a VERB PHRASE with no overt SUBJECT is interpreted as having some subject. For example, in *Susie wants to buy a new car*, the VP *buy a new car* has no overt subject, but we understand that its logical subject is *Susie*, the subject of *wants*, and we call this an instance of SUBJECT CONTROL. But, in *Susie persuaded me to buy a new car*, the understood subject of *buy a new car* is *me*, the object of *persuaded*, and we call this OBJECT CONTROL. Finally, in *Buying a new car is a good idea*, the VP *buying a new car* has no logical subject at all, and we call this ARBITRARY CONTROL.

conversion (also **zero-derivation**) A type of WORD-FORMATION in which a word is shifted from one PART OF SPEECH to another without any additions or changes. For example, the adjective *brown*, as in *a brown skirt*, can be converted into a verb, as in *brown the meat*, and into a noun, as in *The Cleveland Browns traditionally wear brown*, and the noun *smoke*, as in *no smoke without fire*, can be converted into a verb, as in *Susie smokes*, and then back into a noun, as in *Susie was having a smoke.*

cooccurrence restriction Any limitation on the ability of particular words or forms to occur together within a single sentence. A purely grammatical restriction is a DEPENDENCY, while one based on meaning is a SELECTIONAL RESTRICTION. See these entries.

coordinate structure (also **coordination**, **conjunction**) Any grammatical construction in which two or more grammatical units are connected (CONJOINED) with a conjunction like *and, or* or *yet.* Each of the units connected in a coordinate structure is a CONJUNCT (sense 1). In the following examples, the conjuncts are bracketed: *I'm having dinner with* [*Susie*] *and* [*her mother*]; *Would you like* [*coffee*] *or* [*tea?*];

Diamonds are found [*in Russia,*] [*in South Africa*] *and* [*in the Congo*]; *She polished the table* [*lovingly*] *and* [*with great care*].

If the conjunction is *or*, then the whole construction may be called a DISJUNCTION, and each of its conjuncts may be called a DISJUNCT (sense 1).

copula A special item, often a VERB, which serves to connect two parts of a sentence and to express either that the two parts denote the same thing or that the first has the property denoted by the second. The English copula is the verb *be*. The EQUATIONAL SENTENCE *Jan is my girlfriend* asserts that *Jan* and *my girlfriend* are the same person, while the ASCRIPTIVE SENTENCE *Jan is British* assigns the quality of Britishness to *Jan*. See also QUASI-COPULA.

coreference Another term for BINDING; see under ANAPHOR.

corpus A very large body of material produced by the speakers or writers of a particular language, these days typically held on a computer, and available for study. The scrutiny of corpora (this is the plural of *corpus*) has revolutionized both the study of language and the writing of dictionaries, since corpora allow us to obtain large samples of how a language is actually used by its speakers and writers. Linguistic investigations based upon corpora are corpus linguistics.

correlative **1**. A very general term for either a pair of items which work together to connect things in a sentence but are not adjacent. English examples include *both . . . and, either . . . or, neither . . . nor, not only . . . but also, as . . . as, more . . . than, rather . . . than* and *so . . . that.* Examples of use: *I'd rather be lucky than good; Susie both smokes and drinks; This book is so interesting that I can't put it down; Susie earns as much money as Mike does.*

2. In traditional grammar, a generic term including DEMONSTRATIVES, INTERROGATIVES and INDEFINITES. This second sense is now obsolete.

count noun A NOUN denoting something which can be counted, such as *dog, girl, occasion, birthday, link* and *arrival*. Compare MASS NOUN.

counterfactual See under CONDITIONAL SENTENCE.

cranberry morpheme A MORPHEME which occurs in only a single word, such as the *cran-* of *cranberry,* the *twi-* of *twilight* and the *-art* of *braggart.*

D

dangling participle (also **hanging participle**) A PARTICIPLE which is not grammatically linked to the rest of its sentence, or at least not in an orderly manner. For example, in **Driving down the road, a deer leapt out in front of me,* the participial phrase *driving down the road* is dangling: if anything it appears to be linked (wrongly) to *a deer*. In **Having said that, there's another solution*, the participial phrase *having said that* is linked to nothing at all. Though they are not rare in speech, dangling participles are regarded as inappropriate in formal writing, and they should be avoided; they violate the SUBJECT-ATTACHMENT RULE.

dash The punctuation mark [–]. This is used to indicate that a sentence has been broken off without being completed: *General Sedgwick's last words to his worried staff were 'Don't worry boys; they couldn't hit an elephant at this dist– .'* A *pair* of dashes is used to set off a strong interruption to a sentence, one which violently disrupts its flow: *The destruction of Guernica – and there is no doubt that the destruction was deliberate – horrified the world.* For more on its use, see chapter 6 of *The Penguin Guide to Punctuation*. Compare HYPHEN.

dative In some languages with CASE, a case-form used to mark an INDIRECT OBJECT. For example, Basque has the dative case-ending -(*r*)*i*, as in *Liburua Anari eman diot* 'I gave the book to Ana', 'I gave Ana the book'. In traditional grammar, the label *dative* is sometimes applied very loosely to any indirect object, even to the English examples given above as translations.

dative shift A name sometimes given to the construction illustrated by *Susie showed Mike her photos*, as opposed to *Susie showed her photos to Mike*. Only some English verbs permit dative shift: for example, *Susie* *demonstrated her technique to Mike* does not permit **Susie demonstrated Mike her technique*.

declarative The (formal) SENTENCE TYPE commonly used to make a STATEMENT, or the MOOD assigned to a sentence or a verb-form which makes a statement presented as true. English has no special form for this, but the following are examples of declarative sentences: *Susie smokes*; *The war is over*; *Three students failed to sit the examination*; *I am not ready yet*.

declension In a language with CASE, the INFLECTION of a noun or other word for case, or the complete set of inflected forms of such a word, especially when presented as a model for other words showing similar forms. For example, the Latin word *amicus* 'friend' has the following declension:

	Singular	Plural
Nominative	*amicus*	*amici*
Accusative	*amicum*	*amicos*
Genitive	*amici*	*amicorum*
Dative	*amico*	*amicibus*
Ablative	*amico*	*amicibus*

deep structure In TRANSFORMATIONAL GRAMMAR, an abstract structure assigned to a sentence for analytical purposes. The deep structure of a sentence may be quite different from its SURFACE STRUCTURE. For example, the sentence *Jan seems to be happy* may be assigned a deep structure like this: [*Jan to be happy*] *seems*. Most other theories of grammar do not recognize deep structures.

defective Of a particular word, lacking some of the forms which a word of that class normally has. For example, the English verb *must* is defective. It has no past tense: *Today I must pay my bills*, but *Yesterday I ? pay my bills*. It also has no *-ing* form.

defining Another term for RESTRICTIVE.

definite A label applied to a NOUN PHRASE which denotes something which is either already known to the listener or reader or easily identifiable from the context. In the following examples, the bracketed noun phrases are definite. *We interviewed three men and a woman, and we decided to appoint* [*the woman*] (the woman has just been identified by the previous material); [*The moon*] *will rise around midnight* (there is only one moon, and everybody knows about it); *I can't recommend* [*this book*] (I am holding the book up, or pointing at it, or else I identified it a moment ago); [*My mother*] *is ill* (everybody has a mother, and the listener will expect me to have one); *What is* [*the capital of Bulgaria?*] (every country has a capital city); *I took a taxi to their place, but* [*the driver*] *got lost* (every taxi must have a driver). The opposite is INDEFINITE.

definite article A conventional label for the English DETERMINER *the*, or for a similar item in another language.

degree The GRAMMATICAL CATEGORY which expresses the degree to which some quality is present. English ADJECTIVES and ADVERBS commonly distinguish three degrees: the POSITIVE (the basic form), the COMPARATIVE (expressing a higher degree than is present in something else), and the SUPERLATIVE (expressing a maximal degree). The comparative is formed with *-er* or with *more*; the superlative is formed with *-est* or with *most*. Short words like *big* and *fast* tend to prefer *-er* and *-est*; longer ones like *beautiful* and *carefully* take *more* and *most*, though the rules for choosing are a bit complicated. Examples: *Mike is tall; Mike is taller than Ted; Mike is the tallest man I know; Natalie drives carefully; Natalie drives more carefully than Susie; Natalie drives the most carefully of anybody in Sussex.*

Finer distinctions of degree may be made with DEGREE MODIFIERS.

degree modifier That PART OF SPEECH, or a word belonging to this part of speech, which modifies an ADJECTIVE or an ADVERB and expresses the degree to which some quality is present. For example, in the frame *This book is __ expensive*, the blank can be filled by any of various degree modifiers, such as *very, too, so, rather, somewhat, exceedingly, moderately* or *impossibly*. Colloquial English permits some additional degree modifiers, such as *pretty, kind of, sort of, bloody* and a number of rather coarse items. Each of these indicates some degree of expensiveness. Traditional grammars and dictionaries often classify the degree modifiers as a subclass of adverb, but it is probably best to distinguish them.

deictic category Any GRAMMATICAL CATEGORY which 'points' in space or in time. For example, DEICTIC POSITION points in space; TENSE points in time; and PERSON points to the participants in a speech situation.

deictic position The GRAMMATICAL CATEGORY which distinguishes different degrees of distance from the speaker (and, in some languages, also from the hearer). English has a very simple system of deictic position: it distinguishes only a PROXIMAL 'close to the speaker' and a DISTAL 'far from the speaker', as in *this/these* versus *that/those* and *here* versus *there*. Some other languages make more elaborate distinctions, as does Spanish, with its three-way contrast: *aquí* 'here', *allí* 'just there', *ahí* 'over there'.

deixis Linguistic pointing. See DEICTIC CATEGORY.

demonstrative A DETERMINER or a PRONOUN which indicates distance away from the speaker (or, in some languages, from the hearer). English has only a two-way distinction between *this* (plural *these*) (close to the speaker) and *that* (plural *those*) (distant from the speaker). Some other languages make more elaborate distinctions.

deontic modality The area of MOOD or MODALITY concerned with permission, obligation and prohibition. For example, *must* is deontic when it means 'is obliged to', as in *We must finish this job by tomorrow*, and *may* is deontic when it means 'is permitted to', as in *You may use the car tonight*. Compare EPISTEMIC MODALITY.

dependency Any grammatical link between two different items in a sentence. Among the more important dependencies are SUBCATEGORIZATION, AGREEMENT and GOVERNMENT; see those entries.

derivation 1. A type of WORD-FORMATION in which a word is derived from another word by adding an AFFIX. English examples include *writer* and *rewrite* from *write*, *trans-Atlantic* from *Atlantic*, *frosty* and *defrost* from *frost*, and each of the steps involved in *nation* > *national* > *international* > *internationally*. Compare INFLECTION.

2. In TRANSFORMATIONAL GRAMMAR, the series of steps involved in converting a DEEP STRUCTURE into a SURFACE STRUCTURE.

derivational morphology The branch of MORPHOLOGY dealing with DERIVATION (sense 1).

descriptivism The policy of describing the facts of languages as we find them to be spoken, without introducing any value judgements of our own. All serious work in linguistics is descriptivist. Compare PRESCRIPTIVISM.

determiner The PART OF SPEECH, or a word belonging to this class, which typically forms the first element in a NOUN PHRASE and which limits the applicability of that noun phrase in some way. A determiner typically occurs in the blank in an incomplete noun phrase like __ *new book* or __ *new books*. Among them are *the, a(n), this, those, some, many, most, few, all, both, no, several, my* and *your*. Note that possessive items like *my* and *your* are strictly determiners, and not PRONOUNS, since they behave grammatically like determiners, and not like pronouns; nevertheless, some traditionally oriented books still label them (wrongly) as possessive pronouns.

The two English determiners *the* and *a(n)* have rather special functions and are often called ARTICLES: *the* is the DEFINITE ARTICLE and *a(n)* is the INDEFINITE ARTICLE.

Those determiners which indicate something about quantity, like *many, all, both* and *no,* are called QUANTIFIERS. A few linguists prefer to regard the quantifiers as a separate part of speech from determiners, but there is little basis for this.

Sometimes we find two determiners in a single noun phrase: *all my books, both my children*. In this case, the first of the two is often called a PREDETERMINER.

There is disagreement about the classification of the CARDINAL NUMERAL. These often behave like determiners, as in *three new books*. But they also occur together with other determiners, as in *these three new books*. Some linguists therefore regard them as POSTDETERMINERS, another special subclass of determiner.

See also ZERO DETERMINER.

diachronic Pertaining to the time element in language; involving change in a language over time. A diachronic approach to the study of a language is the study of its development over some period of time. Compare SYNCHRONIC.

diacritic (also, informally, **accent**) A mark placed above, below or on top of a letter to indicate something about its pronunciation. English makes only limited use of diacritics, but we sometimes write *Zoë, learnèd* or *Nestlé* to indicate that the marked vowel is a separate syllable. Many other written languages make very heavy use of diacritics.

diaeresis A mark, consisting of two dots placed above a vowel letter, to indicate that the vowel forms a separate syllable, as in *Zoë* or *naïve.*

dialect Any distinctive speech variety associated with the people in a particular geographical region (this is a *regional dialect*) or in a particular social group (this is a *social dialect*, or *sociolect*). English, like most languages, exhibits a number of regional dialects: people from London, Liverpool, Newcastle, Glasgow, New York, Chicago and Sydney (for example) all speak English somewhat differently. There are also social dialects: even in London, a taxi driver does not speak like a stockbroker. Even STANDARD ENGLISH is just one dialect of English, though it is a dialect with a very special status.

Note: in Britain, the term *dialect* denotes only the particular vocabulary and grammatical features of a speech variety, and it excludes accent, a particular type of pronunciation. In the USA, however, an accent is usually considered to be part of a dialect.

digraph A sequence of two letters representing a single sound, such as the *sh* in *fish* or the *th* in *think*.

diminutive (also **hypocoristic**) A modified form of a word which expresses small size, or, sometimes, merely affection. English usually forms diminutives by suffixing *-y* or *-ie*, often to a reduced form of the source word, as in *hanky* for *handkerchief*, *doggie* for *dog* and *Tommie* for *Thomas*. But we also use *-ette*, as in *statuette* and *kitchenette*.

direct object The GRAMMATICAL RELATION which most typically represents the person or thing receiving the action of the verb. In the following examples, the bracketed sequences are prototypical direct objects: *John hit* [*Bill*]; *Tamerlane defeated* [*Sultan Beyazit*]; *Susie painted* [*the bedroom*]. In the following further examples, the bracketed sequences are still grammatically direct objects, even though they are less typical: *Issagonis designed* [*the Mini*]; *Susie spotted* [*an intruder*]; *Susie bid* [*six spades*]; *Mike owns* [*400 board games*]; *Susie has* [*blue eyes*].

direct question A sentence which has the form of a question expecting an answer. Examples: *Are you going to Susie's party?*; *What is the capital of Latvia?*; *How many players are there in a baseball team?* Compare EMBEDDED QUESTION, and see RHETORICAL QUESTION.

direct speech Quoting someone's exact words. In writing, direct speech is enclosed within QUOTATION MARKS. Example: *'I'm fed up', Susie said.* Compare INDIRECT SPEECH.

discontinuous constituent A syntactic unit which is broken up into two separated pieces. Consider the sentence *A student who speaks Chechen turned up this morning.* Here the subject is *a student who speaks Chechen*, and this is a single grammatical unit, a NOUN PHRASE. But it is also possible to say, or write, *A student turned up this morning who speaks Chechen.* Here that noun phrase has been split into two separated pieces, *a student* and *who speaks Chechen*, and it is now a discontinuous constituent.

discourse A connected stretch of language of some size, such as a conversation or a lecture. Some linguists restrict the term to a piece of speech, preferring TEXT for a piece of writing.

discourse marker A word or a phrase which is linked weakly or not at all to an adjoining sentence and which serves chiefly to keep a conversation or a text flowing smoothly. Among the items commonly used in this way are *yes*, *so*, *of course*, *nevertheless*, and, of course, *well.*

disjunct **1**. Any of two or more items connected by *or*, as in *coffee or tea*.

2. In the QUIRK GRAMMARS, another name for a SENTENCE ADVERB, so called because a sentence adverb is very weakly linked grammatically to the rest of its sentence.

disjunction A COORDINATE STRUCTURE involving *or* or *either . . . or*. Examples: *Would you like coffee or tea?*; *On an attempted runout, a cricket umpire may make the call or ask the third umpire to adjudicate*; *The successful applicant will either be a native speaker of French or hold a degree in French*. The items connected by the *or* are DISJUNCTS.

dislocation A construction in which a NOUN PHRASE is moved out of its normal position to the beginning or the end of the sentence, while its normal position is occupied by a PRONOUN. If it is moved to the beginning, we have LEFT-DISLOCATION; if to the end, we have RIGHT-DISLOCATION. Two examples of left-dislocation: *Mike, he's a nice guy*; *Susie, I really like her*. Of right-dislocation: *She's a great person, Susie*; *I really hate it, this takeaway exam*. Compare TOPICALIZATION.

distal See under DEICTIC POSITION.

distribution The set of linguistic contexts in which a linguistic item or class of items can occur. For example, a typical ADJECTIVE can occur in the following contexts, among others: *a very __ book*; *This book is __*; *__ though this book is, it is too expensive*. Distribution is a major criterion in assigning linguistic elements to classes, such as assigning words to PARTS OF SPEECH.

distributive Any linguistic form which picks out the members of a group as individuals. A distributive often involves *each* or *apiece*. Examples: *There's enough wine for two bottles apiece* (every person in the group can have two bottles); *The children each received a present* (there was one present for each child).

ditransitive verb A VERB which takes two objects, such as *give*, *show* and *teach*. In the following examples, the two objects are bracketed: *She gave* [*me*] [*a kiss*]; *She showed* [*her girlfriend*] [*her flat*]; *She taught* [*us*] [*Latin*].

***do*-support** A name sometimes given to the use of the 'dummy' auxiliary *do*, which is used in English when an AUXILIARY is required but no other auxiliary is present. Examples, starting with *Susie smokes*; *Susie doesn't smoke*; *Does Susie smoke?*; *Susie smokes, doesn't she?*

double genitive A name sometimes given to the English construction illustrated by examples like *a friend of mine, a student of Chomsky's* and *that car of John's*. These are used to express the sense of the ungrammatical forms like **my a friend* and **John's that car*.

double negative Any construction in which two or more negative words occur in a single clause. Examples: *I didn't see nothing* (= *I didn't see anything*); *No football team can't win no championship without no defenders* (= *No football team can win a championship without defenders*). Such constructions are normal in most vernacular forms of English, and they were formerly accepted also in standard English, but, for some centuries now, they have been regarded as non-standard. But note that standard English does accept double negatives when both negatives are logically required, as in *You can't not go* (= *It is impossible for you not to go*).

The use of double negatives is called NEGATIVE CONCORD by linguists, and negative concord is standard in some other languages. For example, to express 'I don't regret anything', standard French requires *Je ne regrette rien,* literally 'I don't regret nothing', and, to express 'I didn't see anybody', standard Spanish requires *No he visto a nadie,* literally 'I didn't see nobody'.

It is a common error to suppose that a double negative is equivalent to a positive. For example, *I didn't see nobody* plainly does not mean 'I saw somebody', and nobody but a fool would think that it does. This merely happens to be a non-standard, but perfectly familiar and understandable, way of saying 'I didn't see anybody'.

double passive The construction in which passive verb-forms occur both in a matrix clause and in a complement clause. The result is often clumsy, as in *The city was allowed to be captured.* Sometimes it results in ungrammaticality, as in **The Duke was attempted to be killed.*

double perfect The construction in which two instances of perfect *have* appear within a single sequence of verbs. A typical example is *I would have liked to have seen that.* This construction is usually objectionable: it would be better to write either *I would like to have seen that* or *I would have liked to see that,* depending on whether the liking is in the present or the past. For example, you would write *I would like to have met Napoleon,* since **I would have liked to meet Napoleon* suggests, wrongly, that you had a chance to meet Napoleon, but you might write

I would have liked to marry Gabriella, meaning that marrying Gabriella would have pleased you at the time, though not necessarily now.

dual A grammatical form denoting exactly two of something. English has only a very few dual forms, notably *both*, *either* and *neither* (with more than two, we use *all*, *any* and *none*, respectively).

dummy (also **expletive**) A meaningless word which is grammatically required to fill a position which would otherwise be empty but which refers to nothing. The two common English dummies are *it* and *there*. Examples: *It's raining*; *It's obvious that she's interested*; *There's a wasp on your back*; *There are no tigers in Africa*. In each of these examples, the *it* or *there* refers to nothing at all, but is required to make the sentence grammatical. Compare *They've just had a baby – it's a girl* and *I looked in the bedroom, but I didn't find it there*, in which *it* refers to the baby and *there* means 'in the bedroom'.

The English AUXILIARY *do* is sometimes called a *dummy auxiliary*, since it is required only for grammatical purposes, as in *Mike doesn't smoke* and *Does Mike smoke?*

durative An ASPECT form which indicates that an action or a state of affairs persists unchanged over a period of time. English has no special form for this. In the past tense, we commonly use the simple past, as in *I waited for an hour*.

dvandva A type of COMPOUND in which each element has an equal claim to being considered the HEAD, as though the elements were joined by the word *and*. Examples: *Austria–Hungary*, *tragicomic*, *freeze-dry*.

dynamic (also **eventive**) A label applied to a verb, a verb-form, a predicate or a sentence expressing an action, a movement or a change. Examples: *Jan peeled the potatoes*; *Jan left the room*; *Jan turned bright red*. Compare STATIVE.

E

echo response Any response to an utterance which largely repeats what has just been said. Examples: Susie: *Did you get the coriander?*; Mike: *Did I get what?*; Susie: *I saw Alice this morning*; Mike: *You saw Alice this morning.*

ellipsis The omission from a sentence of material which is logically required to complete its structure. Examples: *'Nough said* ('Enough said'); *Seems we have a problem* ('It seems we have a problem').

embedded question (also indirect question) A QUESTION which is not being asked directly, but which merely forms part of a larger sentence, which itself may or may not be a question. In the following examples, the bracketed sequences are indirect questions. *I don't know* [*what I should do*] (the whole sentence is a statement in which the direct question *What should I do?* is embedded); *Tell me who I should talk to* (a command embedding the direct question *Who should I talk to?*); *Can you tell me where I can find the lost-and-found office?* (a question embedding the direct question *Where can I find the lost-and-found office?*). Note that an embedded question has a different word order from a direct question. An embedded YES–NO QUESTION is introduced by *whether* or *if*: *I don't know if we can afford it* (the embedded question is *Can we afford it?*).

embedding The presence of one CLAUSE inside another, sometimes especially inside another clause of the same kind. Consider the following example: *The critics who declared that the book that I had written was rubbish have been embarrassed.* Here the relative clause *that I had written* is embedded within the larger complement clause *that the book that I had written was rubbish,* which in turn is embedded within the still larger relative clause *who declared that the book that I had written was* *rubbish*, which finally is embedded within the main clause making up the whole sentence. With clauses bracketed, the structure of the whole sentence is this: [*The critics* [*who declared* [*that the book* [*that I had written*] *was rubbish*]] *have been embarrassed*].

emphasis A broad and informal term for any way of attaching particular importance to some part of a sentence or an utterance. Linguists prefer the term FOCUS: see this term for examples.

emphatic stress The addition of stress to a part of a sentence in order to emphasize it. For example, instead of saying *The Scots invented golf*, we can say *The SCOTS invented golf*, with strong stress on *Scots*, in order to emphasize this word.

empty morph A piece of a word which contributes nothing to the meaning of a word but which is required to make the word easily pronounceable. An English example is the *-o-* found in words like *kissogram* (*kiss* plus *-gram*) and *stripogram* (*strip* plus *-gram*).

enclitic See under CLITIC.

endocentric compound A COMPOUND which denotes a particular type of what is denoted by its HEAD. Examples: an *armchair* is a type of chair; *sky-blue* is a kind of blue; and to *spray-paint* is one way to paint. Compare BAHUVRIHI.

epicene In a language with a GENDER system showing a correlation with sex, denoting a noun which is invariable in gender but which can take referents of either sex. For example, French *écrivain* 'writer' and *témoin* 'witness' are always masculine, even when referring to women, while *victime* 'victim' and *personne* 'person' are always feminine, even when referring to men. Compare COMMON GENDER.

epistemic modality The area of MOOD or MODALITY concerned with knowledge and belief. For example, *must* is epistemic when it means 'is undoubtedly', as in (on hearing the doorbell) *That must be Susie*, and *may* is epistemic when it means 'is possibly', as in *We may need some help*. Compare DEONTIC MODALITY.

equational sentence A sentence which asserts that two descriptions or names denote (or do not denote) the same person or thing. Examples: *Tony Blair is the British prime minister; Saturn is not the largest planet; My wife is my best friend.* An equational sentence can be turned around: *My best friend is my wife.* This is one type of copular sentence; compare ASCRIPTIVE SENTENCE.

equative A construction indicating that the DEGREE of one thing is equal to the degree of another thing, usually expressed in English with *as . . . as*, sometimes reinforced with further words like *just* or *every bit.* Examples: *Susie drives as well as I do; Mike is just as good a cook as I am; Susie speaks French every bit as fluently as Ted.*

ergative verb A verb which can be either INTRANSITIVE, in which case the thing undergoing the action is represented by the subject, or TRANSITIVE, in which case the thing undergoing the action is represented by the direct object and the subject denotes the person or thing causing the action. An example is *sink*: *The ship sank; The sub sank the ship.* English has many such verbs; among the others are *melt* (*The ice melted/The sun melted the ice*), *boil, dissolve, explode, freeze* and *collapse.*

The term is inappropriate and unfortunate, since the sense has nothing to do with the grammatical phenomenon linguists call 'ergativity', and it is not usual among linguists, but it has become conventional among teachers of English.

ethical construction Any construction which includes explicit reference to a person who is affected by the action (almost always adversely) but not directly involved in it. The most usual English form for this purpose is the preposition *on* followed by a pronoun. Examples: *The dog died on me; Jane's boyfriend walked out on her; They stole the car on us.*

euphemism A polite word or expression used in place of a blunter one in order to avoid giving offence. Examples include *pass away* for *die, wee* for *urinate* and *make love* for *copulate.*

eventive Another term for DYNAMIC.

exception A form or construction which does not obey the usual rules. English nouns usually form their plurals in *-s*, as with *girls* and *foxes*, but *children* and *teeth* are exceptions. Transitive verbs usually form passives, as in *Susie kissed Natalie* and *Natalie was kissed by Susie*, but *Susie weighs 45 kilos* is an exception, since **45 kilos is weighed by Susie* is not possible.

exclamation An utterance, especially a complete sentence, which expresses strong emotion: one kind of (functional) SENTENCE TYPE. In English, an exclamation usually has a distinctive structure, the EXCLAMATORY sentence type. Examples: *How well Thorpe batted yesterday!*; *What a lovely painting this is!* Compare these with ordinary statements: *Thorpe batted very well yesterday*; *This is a very lovely painting.*

exclamation mark The punctuation mark [!], placed at the end of an utterance which is an EXCLAMATION or which merely expresses strong emotion. Examples: *What a lovely day it is!*; *I can't believe it!* For more on its use, see chapter 2 of *The Penguin Guide to Punctuation*.

exclamatory The (formal) SENTENCE TYPE (or MOOD) represented by the distinctive sentence structure illustrated in *How beautiful it is!* This pattern is commonly used in making an EXCLAMATION.

existential sentence A sentence which asserts the existence or non-existence of something, either in general or in a specified location. English uses its *there is* construction for this purposes. Examples: *There's a wasp on your back*; *There are no tigers in Africa*; *There are billions of galaxies*; *There were no human beings in New Zealand before the Maoris arrived*.

exocentric compound Another term for BAHUVRIHI.

exophor A linguistic item which resembles an ANAPHOR but which points to something in the context in which the speaker finds herself, and not to the linguistic context. For example, if I hold up a book and say *This is a good book*, the item *this* is behaving as an exophor, since there is no earlier linguistic context for it to point to, but only the book in my hand.

expletive **1**. Another term for DUMMY.

2. A swear word, sometimes especially one which is inserted into the middle of a phrase as a meaningless emotional intensifier, as in *Where's that bloody cat?*

external sandhi See under SANDHI.

extraction Another term for an UNBOUNDED DEPENDENCY.

extraposition Any construction in which a (typically long) phrase is removed from its normal position and placed at the end of the sentence. For example, *That she is drunk is obvious* has an extraposed counterpart *It is obvious that she is drunk*. A slightly different example is represented by *A student who speaks Chechen turned up this morning* and its extraposed counterpart *A student turned up this morning who speaks Chechen*.

F

factive verb A VERB which assumes that what follows it is true. For example, *realize* is a factive verb, and so *Susie realized that she had lost her keys* can only be said by someone who believes that it is true that Susie had lost her keys. Not all verbs are factive: *Susie suspected that she had lost her keys* does not assume that Susie had in fact lost her keys.

false friend A word in a foreign language which looks very much like a word in your own language but which has a very different meaning. For example, French *librairie* looks very much like *library*, but it means *bookshop*, and Spanish *competencia* looks like English *competence*, but it means *competition*.

feminine In some languages with GENDER, a gender class which shows some degree of correlation with female sex. Many European languages have such a gender class, but the correlation with female sex is usually rather weak. In French, for example, most nouns denoting females are grammatically feminine, but there are exceptions, such as *soprano* 'soprano', which is grammatically masculine, even though all sopranos are women. In any case, most feminine nouns in French denote things which have no sex at all, such as *maison* 'house', *moûtarde* 'mustard' and *découverte* 'discovery'.

English, of course, has no grammatical gender at all, and words like *she* and *duchess* are marked only for female sex, not for feminine gender.

finite (also **tensed**) A label applied to a verb-form or a clause which is marked for TENSE. With its paucity of verbal inflection, English is not the ideal language to illustrate the distinction between finite and non-finite forms, but here are some examples. In the PRESENT tense, only the third-person singular normally receives an overt marking for tense: the ending *-s*. So, for example, in *Susie smokes*, the verb-form *smokes* is finite. By analogy, then, the form *smoke* is also finite in *I smoke, you smoke* and *Both women smoke*, even though there is no overt marker of tense in these cases. In contrast, the identical-looking form *smoke* is not finite in cases like *You may smoke* and *Susie wants to smoke*, where *smoke* is the INFINITIVE. In the PAST tense in English, tense is marked rather more systematically, either by the ending *-ed* or by a change in the stem of the verb: *Susie enjoyed her holiday* (here *enjoyed* is finite); *Susie took her niece to the beach* (here *took*, the past tense of *take*, is finite). The opposite is NON-FINITE.

first-person The PERSON category which denotes the speaker and possibly also some people associated with the speaker. The English first-person PRONOUNS are *I/me* (singular) and *we/us* (plural). The singular pronoun *I/me* always means 'the speaker', as in *I need a holiday*. The plural pronoun *we/us* usually means 'the speaker plus somebody else associated with the speaker', as in *The boss wants us to finish this report by Friday*. In rare circumstances, *we/us* can mean 'the speakers', as when an American football crowd chant *We want a touchdown!*

flection An old-fashioned term for INFLECTION.

floating quantifier A QUANTIFIER which occurs later in a sentence than in its logical position. For example, instead of saying *All the students have submitted their essays*, we can say *The students have all submitted their essays*, in which the quantifier *all* has 'floated' away from its logical position.

focus That part of a sentence which represents the most important new information. Consider the sentence *Jan bought Larry a shirt*. Here nothing is obviously in focus. But we can place any part of the sentence into focus in speech by stressing it: *JAN bought Larry a shirt* (it was Jan, not somebody else, who bought it); *Jan BOUGHT Larry a shirt* (she got it by paying for it, not otherwise); *Jan bought LARRY a shirt* (the shirt was for Larry, not for someone else); *Jan bought Larry A SHIRT* (not a tie or a book). We can also focus on an element with a CLEFT construction: *It was a shirt that Jan bought Larry* (not a tie or a book).

folk etymology The process in which a word of obscure formation is altered in form in order to make it seemingly more transparent, if not always sensible. English examples include *Welsh rabbit* to *Welsh rarebit* (the motivation for *rabbit* is obscure), French *écrevisse* to *crayfish* (a crayfish is not a fish, but at least it lives in the water), and *asparagus* to regional *sparrowgrass* (asparagus is not grass, but at least it's a green plant).

foreign plural A PLURAL form of a NOUN which is not formed according to any native pattern, but which has been imported directly from a foreign language. English has dozens of these. Examples include *radii* for *radius* (from Latin), *phenomena* for *phenomenon* (from Greek), *concerti* for *concerto* (from Italian) and *kibbutzim* for *kibbutz* (from Hebrew). These often cause difficulties for English-speakers, who may have trouble remembering which form is the singular and which is the plural.

form The internal structure, or the physical shape, of a linguistic element, without regard for any meaning or function it may have.

formal **1**. Pertaining to FORM. For example, English makes a formal difference between *hung* and *hanged*, as in *We hung the picture in the lounge* and *We hanged the murderer in Tombstone*.

2. The label applied to an approach to the description of grammar which is fully explicit and mechanical, and often somewhat mathematical in appearance. For example, the statement S → NP VP is a formal way of saying 'A sentence may consist of a noun phrase followed by a verb phrase.' Formalisms of this type are much used in modern grammatical description and theory.

formative A grammatical MORPHEME. English examples include the past-tense marker *-ed* of *She played well*, the plural *-s* of *a swarm of bees* and the possessive *-'s* of *I met Susie's girlfriend*.

fragment An incomplete piece of a SENTENCE, used by itself. Fragments are normal and very frequent in speech. In each of the following exchanges, Mike's response is a fragment. Ted: *Where's Susie?* Mike: *In the library*. Ted: *Can England win the World Cup?* Mike: *Probably not*. In formal writing, however, fragments are usually out of place.

free morpheme A MORPHEME which can possibly stand alone to make a word all by itself, even though it may sometimes combine with other morphemes in a larger word. For example, the English morpheme *happy* is free, because it can stand alone to make the word *happy*, even though it can also combine with other morphemes to make larger words like *unhappy* and *happiness*. Compare BOUND MORPHEME.

free relative (also **headless relative**) A RELATIVE CLAUSE which has no HEAD and which occupies a noun-phrase position all by itself. In the following examples, the free relatives are bracketed: *[What we need] is a hot-air gun; [Whoever did this] is in trouble; We talked about [when we should retire]*. As you can see, an English free relative begins with a WH-word. In each case, there is an alternative which is an ordinary relative clause. In my examples, these would be *the thing that we need, the person who did this* and *the time when we should retire*.

Note that, in English, a free relative sometimes looks just like an EMBEDDED QUESTION. Consider the example *I saw what she put in the box*. When this means 'I saw the thing that she put in the box', it is a free relative. But, when it means 'I can answer the question "What did she put in the box?" ', it is an embedded question.

fronting (also **preposing**) Any construction in which an element of a sentence which would commonly occur somewhere else is placed at the beginning of the sentence. For example, *There was a spider in the bath* has a fronted counterpart *In the bath there was a spider*, in which the prepositional phrase *in the bath* has been fronted. Likewise, *I have seldom seen such a mess* has a fronted counterpart *Seldom have I seen such a mess*, in which the adverb *seldom* is fronted; in this case, the auxiliary verb *have* must also be placed before the subject *I*. Finally, *I can't recommend this book* has a fronted counterpart *This book I can't recommend*, in which the direct object noun phrase *this book* is fronted; this last is TOPICALIZATION.

full stop (also **period**) The PUNCTUATION MARK [.]. In writing, this is placed at the end of a SENTENCE which expresses a statement. See almost any sentence in this book for an example. The full stop is also used in writing certain ABBREVIATIONS, such as *oz.* for *ounce(s)*, *Prof.* for *Professor*, *i.e.* for *in other words*, and *e.g.* for *for example*. See chapters 2 and 7 of *The Penguin Guide to Punctuation* for further information.

function A purpose to which a linguistic form or construction may be put. In linguistic analysis, it is essential to distinguish between form and function: these do not match up one to one, and often a single form can be used in several different functions, while a single function can be served by several different forms. For example, if I want to get somebody to sit down, I can use any of several formally quite different constructions: a command (*Sit down!*), a question (*Why don't you sit down?*), or even a statement (*You can sit down, you know*).

functional grammar Any approach to grammatical description which attaches great importance to the purposes to which grammatical forms are put, and not only to the forms themselves. A number of functional approaches have been developed; one of the most prominent is SYSTEMIC GRAMMAR.

function word Another term for GRAMMATICAL WORD.

fusion The grammatical phenomenon in which two or more morphemes are combined into a larger unit in such a way that no clear boundaries are visible between the morphemes. For example, in English, {foot} plus {Plural} yields *feet*, in which the two morphemes have fused into a single form. In the same way, {take} plus {Past} yields *took*.

future A TENSE which chiefly correlates with time later than the time of speaking. Romance languages like French, Spanish and Italian have a distinct future tense, though they do not always use their future tense for talking about future time. For example, 'I'm going to sing tonight' would in Spanish usually be expressed with present-tense *Voy a cantar esta noche*, not with future *Cantaré esta noche*. English, like most Germanic and Slavic languages, has no future tense at all. We have many ways of talking about future time, but all involve PRESENT-tense forms: *I go to London tomorrow, I'm going to London tomorrow, I'm going to go to London tomorrow, I'll go to London tomorrow, I must go to London tomorrow, I may go to London tomorrow*, and others. All of these express different views of a future event, but not one is a future tense.

future-in-the-past A VERB-form with the following interpretation: at some point in the past, the action is viewed as lying in the future.

Suppose that, last Tuesday, you said this: *Susie is going to quit her job*. Today you might say the following: *Susie was going to quit her job*. This last is a future-in-the-past.

future perfect A VERB-form which indicates that something which is in the future now will be in the past at some point in the future. English uses *will have* or *shall have* to express this. For example, if I say *I will have finished my essay by Friday*, this means that the essay is not finished now, but that I will finish it on or before Friday, so that on Friday I will be able to say *I have finished my essay*.

G

gap The missing grammatical unit in an example of GAPPING.

gapping The construction in which a unit of a sentence is omitted, rather than repeated. Here is an example, in which the gapped unit is represented by *e*: *Jan ordered vegetable pathia and Larry* e *chicken dhansak*. Here the gap *e* represents a silent repetition of *ordered*. It is possible to have more than one gap in a single sentence: *Rod gave the museum a T-shirt and Elton* e e *a pair of glasses*. Here the two gaps represent *gave* and *the museum*.

gender A phenomenon found in some languages, though not in all, in which all NOUNS are divided into two or more classes requiring different AGREEMENT. French, for example, has two gender classes, traditionally called 'masculine' and 'feminine', though the labels are not entirely appropriate. In French, 'an old book' is *un vieux livre*, while 'an old house' is *une vieille maison*. Here both the determiner meaning 'the' and the adjective meaning 'old' vary in form according to the gender of the noun: masculine for *livre* 'book', feminine for *maison* 'house'. Spanish and Italian are similar to French, while German, Russian and Latin have three genders called 'masculine', 'feminine' and 'neuter'.

It is important to realize that gender is not the same thing as sex. In French, for example, gender has only a weak connection with sex: masculine nouns like *oiseau* 'bird', *vin* 'wine' and *soprano* 'soprano' have no particular connection with male sex, and feminine nouns like *moutarde* 'mustard', *découverte* 'discovery' and *sentinelle* 'sentry' have no particular connection with female sex.

In some other gender languages, gender exhibits no connection with sex at all. For example, the African language Swahili has eight genders, none of which shows any connection with sex, while the American language Navaho has at least ten genders, none of which has any connection with sex. In these other languages, gender is sometimes correlated with other categories, such as animacy, size or shape.

English, of course, has no grammatical gender at all. The familiar distinction among *he*, *she* and *it* is a matter of biology, not of gender. It is an error to speak of the difference between *he* and *she* as one of gender, or the difference between *duke* and *duchess*, or the difference between *Robert* and *Roberta*. These are purely distinctions of sex, not of gender.

generative grammar A kind of formal grammar of a language which is capable of listing all and only the grammatical sentences of that language in a purely mechanical way. That is, once a generative grammar has been constructed, it simply defines all the sentences of a language in a mindless, mechanical way, with no further human intervention, much as an algebraic equation defines all the points lying on a particular curve. The idea of generative grammars was introduced into linguistics by the American linguist Noam Chomsky in the 1950s; since then, Chomsky and others have developed and elaborated dozens of different kinds of generative grammars, the most famous being Chomsky's own TRANSFORMATIONAL GRAMMAR. But every kind of generative grammar requires a LEXICON (a set of words) and a set of rules for combining those words into permissible sentences, and generative grammars chiefly differ in the nature of the rules used and in the way the lexicon is organized. Generative grammars are of little or no use in the everyday study of language or grammar for most practical purposes, but they are often of great importance in addressing certain theoretical questions and in constructing computer programs intended to perform real-world tasks with language data.

Note that, in recent years, Chomsky and his followers have been applying the term *generative grammar* rather loosely to the kind of grammatical theorizing which they embrace, even though this work is no longer generative in the original sense of the term.

generic A NOUN OR A NOUN PHRASE which denotes an entire class of things, rather than picking out an individual thing. Most ordinary nouns are generic in isolation: *dog, girl, wine, mystery, happiness*. Generic noun phrases can take any of several forms: *Dogs are closely related to wolves; The dog is closely related to the wolf; A dog is closely related to a wolf.*

genitive Another term for POSSESSIVE, often especially in a language which has a special CASE-form for this function.

gerund A form of a VERB which retains verbal properties but which turns the entire VERB PHRASE containing it into a NOUN PHRASE. In English, the gerund ending is *-ing*. Consider the verb *have*, and consider this example: *I enjoy having a drink in my hand*. Here *have* stands in its gerund form *having*, and *having* is exhibiting verbal properties: in this case, it takes the object *a drink*. The entire verb phrase *having a drink in my hand* is a noun phrase functioning as the object of the verb *enjoy*. In English, a verb phrase headed by a gerund can occupy any noun-phrase position. It can be a subject (*Killing foxes is a horrible pastime*), a direct object (as in the first example), a predicate nominal (*Edward's idea of foreplay is taking his socks off*), or the object of a preposition (*I don't believe in buying wine as an investment*). Compare VERBAL NOUN, and note the discussion there about distinguishing a verbal noun in *-ing* from a gerund.

***get*-passive** See under PASSIVE VOICE.

given and new One way of analysing the structure of a sentence, in terms of its information structure. Many (not all) sentences can be divided into two parts: one part expressing information already known to the hearer (the *given* or *old* information), and a second part expressing information which is not already known (the *new* information). Usually the given part comes first. For example, if I am giving a lecture on the geography of Africa, I might say *Africa has three major deserts*. Here *Africa* is the given information, while *has three major deserts* is the new information.

gnomic The ASPECT category of a statement which expresses a general or timeless truth. English generally uses the simple present for this purpose: *Water boils at 100°C; Rhubarb leaves are poisonous*.

goal The SEMANTIC ROLE which represents the person or place toward which some action is directed, such as *Susie* in *I'm sending Susie some flowers*.

government The grammatical phenomenon in which the *presence* of one item determines the *form* of another item linked to it. For example, in English any preposition requires its object to stand in the objective form if it is a pronoun: *with her*, not **with she*; *to us*, not **to we*; *between you and me*, not **between you and I*. We say that an English preposition *governs* objective case. Compare AGREEMENT.

Government-and-Binding Theory (also **principles-and-parameters approach**) A theory of grammar developed by Noam Chomsky and his colleagues in the 1980s, the direct successor of TRANSFORMATIONAL GRAMMAR.

gradable Of an ADJECTIVE or ADVERB, denoting a property which can be present to a greater or lesser degree. Gradable words permit DEGREE MODIFIERS like *more, most, very* and *rather*. Examples include *big* (*bigger*), *beautiful* (*most beautiful*), *slowly* (*very slowly*) and *interesting* (*rather interesting*). Not all adjectives and adverbs can do this: *alive* (**most alive*), *principal* (**very principal*), *topmost* (**rather topmost*), *immediately* (**very immediately*).

grammar **1**. The branch of linguistics dealing with the structures of words and sentences, commonly divided into MORPHOLOGY (word structure) and SYNTAX (sentence structure).

2. Any particular approach to this study. This is the sense found in labels like TRADITIONAL GRAMMAR and TRANSFORMATIONAL GRAMMAR.

3. A particular description of the grammatical facts of a language.

4. A book containing such a description.

grammatical **1**. Pertaining to GRAMMAR, especially in sense 1.

2. Another term for WELL-FORMED.

grammatical category Any category whose presence causes the words in a particular PART OF SPEECH to vary in form for grammatical reasons. Examples include PERSON, NUMBER, DEGREE, CASE and TENSE, though others exist. In English, pronouns distinguish person (*I, you, she*); nouns distinguish number (*dog/dogs*); adjectives distinguish degree (*big/bigger/biggest*); some pronouns distinguish case (*I/me*); and verbs distinguish tense (*take/took*). Compare SYNTACTIC CATEGORY.

grammatical morpheme A MORPHEME which has little or no meaning but which serves a grammatical function. English examples include *of*, *the*, the plural suffix *-s* and the past-tense suffix *-ed*. Compare LEXICAL MORPHEME.

grammatical relation Any one of the ways in which a NOUN PHRASE can be related to the rest of its sentence. Among the familiar grammatical relations are SUBJECT, DIRECT OBJECT, INDIRECT OBJECT and OBLIQUE OBJECT.

grammatical word (also **function word**) A word which has little or no meaningful content, but which has a grammatical function. English examples include *the*, *of*, *and* and the infinitival *to*. The preposition *to* is grammatical in *Jan gave her magazines to Pete*, as shown by the fact that it can be omitted without loss of meaning in the alternative *Jan gave Pete her magazines*.

greengrocer's apostrophe The non-standard use of the APOSTROPHE in writing a PLURAL, often seen in public signs like *Pizza's £2.99*. Standard English orthography does not normally permit apostrophes in plurals, and would require *Pizzas £2.99*.

group genitive The English construction in which the possessive *-'s* is added to the end of a NOUN PHRASE whose final word is not its HEAD. Examples include *The Queen of England's ancestors* (the ancestors belong to the Queen, not to England), *The Wife of Bath's Tale* (the tale belongs to the wife, not to Bath), and *the woman you were talking to's husband* (the husband belongs to the woman, not to the grammatical word *to*).

H

habitual A particular ASPECT form, a variety of the IMPERFECTIVE, which indicates that the action named is customary, habitual or usual. Some languages have a specialized auxiliary verb for expressing habitual aspect, as does Spanish, with its verb *soler*. English has no such verb, and it expresses habitual aspect variously. In the present tense, the SIMPLE PRESENT form is used: *Susie smokes*; *I get up at 7.30*; *Koalas eat eucalyptus leaves*. Indeed, this is by far the most frequent function of the simple present. In the past tense, we most commonly use our *used to* construction: *Susie used to smoke*; *I used to get up at 7.30*; *Baseball games used to be played in the daytime*. This last often indicates that what was true in the past is no longer true today, but not necessarily so: if I have lost touch with Susie, then *Susie used to smoke* may be consistent with 'and she still does, for all I know'. But sometimes the past habitual is expressed with the simple past: *The Romans wore togas*; *Huge sabre-toothed cats ranged over Kansas at that time*; *The Mogul emperors practised Islam*.

hanging participle Another term for DANGLING PARTICIPLE.

haplology The process in which one of two consecutive identical or similar syllables is lost. For example, *library* is often pronounced in Britain as though it were *libry*, with loss of the first of the two syllables starting with /r/.

head That element in a PHRASE which determines the nature of the phrase. For example, the phrase *the little girl in the blue dress* clearly denotes a kind of girl, and not a kind of dress or a kind of blue. It is therefore a NOUN PHRASE, and its head is *girl*. Similarly, the phrase *as blue as the sky* denotes a kind of blue, and it is an ADJECTIVE PHRASE with the head *blue*.

headless compound Another term for BAHUVRIHI.

headless relative clause Another term for FREE RELATIVE.

headline language The rather special variety of English used in writing newspaper headlines. In the following examples, the first form illustrates headline language and the second ordinary English: *President denies misconduct* (*The President has denied misconduct*); *Universities feeling the pinch* (*Universities are feeling the pinch*); *PM to visit China* (*The Prime Minister is going to visit China*). Compare BLOCK LANGUAGE.

headword (also **lemma**) A word which is a main entry in a dictionary.

hedge An expression used to reduce your commitment to what you are saying, such as *I think, I suppose, I fancy, I would guess, I take it* or *it seems to me*.

helping verb Another term for AUXILIARY.

historic present The use of the PRESENT tense in a narrative.

homograph One of two or more words of different meaning which are spelled in the same way, regardless of whether they are pronounced the same or differently. For example, *bear* (the name of the large animal) and *bear* (the verb, as in *I can't bear this*) are homographs which are pronounced identically, while *lead* (the name of the metal) and *lead* (the verb, as in *The Mayor will lead the parade*) are homographs which are pronounced differently. Compare HOMOPHONE.

homonym A cover term including both HOMOPHONE and HOMOGRAPH.

homophone One of two or more words of different meaning which are pronounced in the same way, regardless of whether they are spelled the same or differently. For example, *bear* (the name of the large animal) and *bear* (the verb, as in *I can't bear this*) are homophones which are spelled the same, while *bare* ('naked') is a further homophone which is spelled differently. Compare HOMOGRAPH.

hortative A traditional label for a construction expressing an exhortation, represented in English by the *let's* construction, as in *Let's go* and *Let's see what's going on.*

hybrid A word constructed by combining MORPHEMES deriving ultimately from different languages. A familiar example is *television*, in which *tele-* 'far' derives from Greek while *vision* 'seeing' derives from Latin. Pedants sometimes object to such hybrid formations, but these are so well-established and so numerous that it is pointless to object to them: *speedometer* (English plus Greek), *megastar* (Greek plus English), *drinkable* (English plus French), *high school* (English plus Greek/Latin), and so on. New hybrids are coined freely: I recently encountered *techno-anorak* 'computer nerd', which elements derive from Greek and from an Eskimo language.

hypercorrection A mistake resulting from a confused attempt at avoiding another mistake. Here is an example. In many vernacular forms of English, it is normal to say *Him and me were there*, but standard English requires *He and I were there*. Vernacular speakers who have been taught to avoid their normal form may overcompensate by saying *This job was done by he and I*, even though standard English requires *by him and me*: this is hypercorrection.

hyphen The punctuation mark [-], which is shorter than a DASH. The hyphen has the following uses.

1. It must be used within a compound modifier, a phrase of two or more words which modifies a following noun. Examples: *a copper-producing region, a low-scoring match, her Swiss-German ancestry, her new-found freedom, a green-eyed beauty, a good-morning kiss, a salt-and-pepper moustache, a ten-year-old son.*

2. It may optionally be used in any COMPOUND word which would be hard to read without it. Examples: *land-owners, bounty-hunter, brick-red.* Often a white space is an alternative here.

3. It must be used after a PREFIX if the whole word would otherwise be hard to read. Examples: *pre-war, mini-computer, anti-vivisectionist, re-cover* ('put a new cover on'; compare *recover* 'get back').

4. It must be used, at the appropriate end, whenever a piece of a word is cited. Examples: *the prefix* re-, *the past-tense suffix* -ed, *pre- and post-war Berlin.*

5. It must be used whenever a word is broken at the end of a line.

For more information on the hyphen, see *The Penguin Guide to Punctuation*, section 6.1.

The hyphen should not be confused with the dash, and it should never follow a COLON.

hypocoristic Another term for DIMINUTIVE.

hypotaxis Another term for SUBORDINATION.

I

idiom A fixed expression whose meaning is not guessable from the meanings of its parts. Examples include *let the cat out of the bag* (reveal a secret), *buy a pig in a poke* (commit oneself to a course of action without investigating), *a fish out of water* (a person struggling in an unfamiliar environment) and *kick the bucket* (die).

ill-formed (also **ungrammatical**) Of a sentence, not constructed in accordance with the grammatical rules of the language; not WELL-FORMED. All of the following are ill-formed in standard English, and probably in all varieties of English: **These dog are hungry*; **New book this is interesting*; **Susie wants buy a car*. The next examples, however, are ill-formed in standard English but well-formed in certain regional and social varieties of English: **NYPD Blue is a poor show any more*; **I ain't seen him today*; **I might could do it*; **Us is happy about it*.

In educational contexts, we are normally concerned only with well-formedness and ill-formedness in standard English, but even this issue is not always straightforward: see USAGE.

immediate constituent See under CONSTITUENT STRUCTURE.

imperative The (formal) SENTENCE TYPE (or MOOD) illustrated in English by the following distinctive sentence pattern: *Wash your hands!* This pattern commonly expresses a COMMAND. In English, an imperative usually has no overt subject (though *you* is understood as its subject), and the verb stands in its INFINITIVE (uninflected) form. In writing, an imperative is often punctuated with an EXCLAMATION MARK. Examples: *Wash the dishes!*; *Do your homework!*; *Don't smoke in the house!* It is possible, however, to put *you* into subject position, as in *You watch your mouth, young lady!*

It is best to reserve the label *imperative* for a sentence which has this form. It is possible, and normal, in English to use an imperative sentence for a function other than giving a command. For example, if you are going out to a film, I may say *Enjoy the film*, but this is not an order, only a hope. And, if we are following a recipe that calls for caraway seeds, and we've run out of them, I can say *Try cumin seeds*, and this is not an order, but a suggestion.

Likewise, it is possible to use another sentence form to give an order. Most obviously, an army officer can say to his men *I order you to hold your position*. This is certainly an order, yet it does not have the form of an imperative sentence: instead, it has the form of a DECLARATIVE sentence. Compare JUSSIVE.

imperfect A particular set of verb-forms, found in Romance languages like Spanish, French and Italian. The imperfect is PAST in tense and IMPERFECTIVE in aspect, and so it usually denotes an action which extended over a period of time in the past. There is no single English equivalent: for example, Spanish *bebía* may be translated as 'I was drinking', 'I used to drink' or even (in certain circumstances) 'I drank'.

imperfective The ASPECT category which indicates that the action of a verb is presented as having internal structure. The most familiar varieties of the imperfective in English are the CONTINUOUS and the HABITUAL. For example, corresponding to the perfective form *Susie drank vodka*, which expresses no internal structure, we have continuous *Susie was drinking vodka* and habitual *Susie used to drink vodka*, as well as other possibilities like the ITERATIVE *Susie kept (on) drinking vodka*. Compare PERFECTIVE.

impersonal A very general label for any construction in which the action described is assigned to no one in particular. English often uses the 'dummy' pronoun *it* for this purpose: *It is raining; It seems that we have a problem; It transpired that the councillors had been fiddling their expenses; It so happened that there was a doctor in the audience*. But other constructions exist: impersonal *they* in *A delicatessen is a place where they sell specialist foods*, impersonal *you* in *A delicatessen is a place where you buy specialist foods*, and impersonal *one*, as in *One must be very careful*. See also IMPERSONAL PASSIVE.

impersonal passive A sentence in the PASSIVE VOICE which attributes the action of the verb to no one in particular. In English, impersonal passives often begin with the dummy *it*: *it is thought that . . .* , *it is believed that . . .* , *it is said that . . .* Example: *It is often said that Basque is an exceedingly difficult language to learn.*

inalienable possession The property of a POSSESSIVE in which the possessed represents something that cannot reasonably be separated from the possessor. Examples: *Susie's parents, my eyes, Susie's name, France's history*. Unlike some other languages, English makes no distinction of form between this and ALIENABLE POSSESSION.

inanimate The label applied to a NOUN or a NOUN PHRASE which denotes something other than a human being or an animal. Plants, though living, are classed as inanimate. Examples: *tree, index, absence, my ancestry, the capital of Italy, the rest of the book*. Compare ANIMATE.

inchoative The ASPECT category which indicates that something is just beginning. Unlike some other languages, English has no particular form for this. We use a verb like *start* or *begin*, as in *It started to rain*.

incorporation The grammatical pattern in which a noun is combined with a verb to produce a complex verb. Incorporation is not common in English, but we do have complex verbs like *babysit* ('sit with a baby'), *house-hunt* ('hunt for a house') and *stargaze* ('gaze at stars').

indefinite A very general label applied to any linguistic form which refers to nobody and nothing in particular. English has the INDEFINITE ARTICLE *a*(*n*), several INDEFINITE PRONOUNS like *something* and *anybody*, and various other indefinite forms like *somewhere, somehow* and the *ever* of *Have you ever been in Paris?*

indefinite article The conventional name for the English determiner *a* (or *an*). This has two distinct uses. For example, *I'm looking for a house* can mean either 'I'm looking for a specific house (of which I know the identity but you don't)' or 'I'm looking for some house or other (perhaps one suitable for buying)'. The first is called the *specific* sense, the second the *non-specific sense*. Compare DEFINITE ARTICLE.

indefinite pronoun A PRONOUN which denotes nobody in particular. The English indefinite pronouns are *somebody, someone, something, anybody, anyone* and *anything*. The negative pronouns (*nobody, no one, nothing*) are sometimes also classed as indefinite pronouns.

indicative The MOOD category associated with an ordinary statement: *My wife is away; We have just returned from Prague; Oil is not soluble in water; Susie will be back shortly*. In English, as in most languages, the indicative has no special marking.

indirect object In traditional grammar, the GRAMMATICAL RELATION borne by a noun phrase which represents a grammatical OBJECT, distinct from a DIRECT OBJECT, which identifies the person or people indirectly affected by the action of the verb. Consider the sentences *Mike gave the books to Susie* and *Mike gave Susie the books*. Traditionally, *Susie* would be classed as an indirect object in both cases, contrasting with the subject *Mike* and the direct object *the books*. However, not all contemporary linguists would agree: in the first example, *Susie* looks very much like an ordinary object of a preposition, while, in the second, the existence of the passive *Susie was given the books by Mike* suggests that *Susie* is really a direct object. It is therefore not certain that English has any indirect objects, and different linguists hold varying views on the issue.

indirect question Another term for EMBEDDED QUESTION.

indirect speech (also **reported speech**) Reporting what someone has said without quoting the exact words. Example: *Susie said she was fed up*. Compare DIRECT SPEECH.

infinitive A particular verb-form, occurring in some but not all languages, which serves to express the verbal idea in its simplest form, without any marking for tense, aspect, mood, person or other grammatical categories. In English, the infinitive is the bare form of a verb, its dictionary form, the form which can immediately follow a MODAL AUXILIARY like *must* or *will* or which can follow the 'infinitival' particle *to*: *go, sleep, take, be, arrive, consider, decide* and so on. Because of the confusion noted in the next paragraph, this form is sometimes called the *bare infinitive* or the *base form*.

However, as a result of confusion, many people have gained the false impression that the infinitive of a verb consists of the bare infinitive preceded by the particle *to*, and as a result they believe that infinitives are forms like *to go*, *to sleep* and *to take*. This view is mistaken: that *to* does not form part of the verb at all, as is shown, for example, by the fact that *to* can readily be separated from a following infinitive by a phrase, as explained under SPLIT INFINITIVE. Still, this erroneous view is prominent, and therefore we sometimes find it convenient to speak of a sequence like *to go* as a TO-INFINITIVE.

infix An AFFIX which interrupts another MORPHEME. English has no true infixes, but the plural suffix *-s* behaves something like an infix in unusual plurals like *passers-by* and *mothers-in-law*.

inflection Changes in the form of a word for grammatical reasons. For example, the noun *dog* has just two inflected forms, *dog* and *dogs*, while the verb *take* has the five inflected forms *take, takes, took, taking* and *taken*. Compare DERIVATION (sense 1).

inflectional morphology The branch of MORPHOLOGY dealing with the way in which words (LEXICAL ITEMS) change their forms for grammatical purposes. For example, *dog* may appear as either *dog* or *dogs*, depending on the context; *big* may appear as any of *big, bigger* or *biggest*; and *write* may appear as any of *write, writes, wrote, writing* or *written*. Compare DERIVATIONAL MORPHOLOGY.

initialism A word constructed by taking the initial letters of the important words in a phrase, producing something which cannot be pronounced as a word, but must be spelled out letter by letter. Examples: *BBC* (for *British Broadcasting Corporation*), *FBI* (for *Federal Bureau of Investigation*). Compare ACRONYM. Note that some people do not distinguish initialisms from acronyms, using *acronym* for both.

instrument The SEMANTIC ROLE which expresses the object with which some task is performed, such as *an old toothbrush* in *She scrubbed her brooch with an old toothbrush*. English usually expresses an instrument with the preposition *with*, as in the example, though occasionally it uses *by*, as in *She wrote this by hand*. Some other languages, such as Russian and Basque, have a distinct CASE-form for instruments, the *instrumental* case.

instrumental A label applied to a NOUN PHRASE which denotes the instrument or means with which some task is performed. English commonly uses the preposition *with* for this purpose: *She writes her letters with a fountain pen*. But other prepositions are sometimes possible: *I wrote this book on my Mac; I wrote this book in WordPerfect.*

intensifier Another (and rather inaccurate) term for DEGREE MODIFIER.

intensive reflexive A REFLEXIVE PRONOUN which does not occupy its own slot in the sentence but serves only to emphasize a noun phrase which is already present. An example is *myself* in *I myself did it* or *I did it myself*. These are merely emphatic ways of saying *I did it*, and they are different from a true REFLEXIVE, like *I saw myself in the mirror*.

interfix A piece of meaningless material inserted between a STEM and an AFFIX to produce a result which is easier to pronounce. An English example is the *-o-* which appears in formations like *kissogram* (*kiss* plus *-gram*) and *stripogram* (*strip* plus *-gram*).

interjection A word or phrase which, as a rule, occurs by itself, expresses emotion and does not form part of a sentence. English examples include *Ouch!*, *Damn!*, *Aaargh!*, *Whoopee!*, *My god!* and *Bloody hell!*, as well as a number of coarser expressions.

internal sandhi See under SANDHI.

interrogative The MOOD category assigned to a QUESTION, or the (formal) SENTENCE TYPE commonly employed for this purpose. Unlike some other languages, English has no special marking for questions, but we do construct most questions with a distinctive word order. Compare the word order of the (INDICATIVE) statement *Susie is drinking tea* with the word order of the YES–NO QUESTION *Is Susie drinking tea?* and the WH-QUESTION *What is Susie drinking?* Here both questions exhibit INVERSION.

interrogative pronoun A PRONOUN which asks a question. The English ones are *who*, *what* and *which*, as in these examples: *Who were you talking to?*; *What happened?*; *Which do you prefer?*

intransitive The label applied to a VERB which does not take a DIRECT OBJECT. Some English verbs are always intransitive and can never take an object; among these are *arrive, snore, elapse, hibernate* and *stroll*:

Susie arrived early.	**Susie arrived the party early.*
Susie was snoring.	**Susie was snoring a racket.*
Two hours elapsed.	**Two hours elapsed my attention.*
Bears hibernate.	**Bears hibernate the winter.*
Susie strolled along the shore.	**Susie strolled the kids along the shore.*

Many other verbs can be either transitive or intransitive; see LABILE VERB. Compare TRANSITIVE. The label *intransitive* is also applied to a verb phrase or a clause containing an intransitive verb.

Note that certain intransitive verbs can be followed by NOUN PHRASES which are not direct objects. For examples of these, see COPULA and QUASI-COPULA.

inversion Any construction in which the ordinary WORD ORDER is reversed, and particularly a case in which the order of the SUBJECT and an AUXILIARY verb is reversed (this is SUBJECT-VERB INVERSION). Consider the statement *Susie is buying a car*, in which the subject *Susie* precedes the auxiliary *is*. In the corresponding YES-NO QUESTION *Is Susie buying a car?*, the order of these two elements is inverted, and the same is true in the WH-QUESTION *What car is Susie buying?* Inversion also occurs in certain other circumstances. For example, *I have often wondered about that* undergoes FRONTING to produce *Often I have wondered about that*, but *I have seldom seen such a mess* has the fronted version *Seldom have I seen such a mess*, with inversion of *I* and *have*.

inverted commas Another name for QUOTATION MARKS.

irrealis A very general label for any grammatical form or construction which expresses some kind of unreality. English has no very systematic way of expressing unreality, but the irrealis is clearly expressed in COUNTERFACTUAL sentences; see under CONDITIONAL SENTENCE.

irregular A label applied to any linguistic item which does not behave in the way that is typical of items in its class. For example, the verb *watch* is REGULAR (*I watch her, I watched her, I have watched her*), while *see* is irregular (*I see her, I saw her, I have seen her*).

***it*-cleft** See under CLEFT.

iterative An ASPECT form, a variety of the IMPERFECTIVE, which indicates that an action is repeated a number of times. In English, the iterative is usually expressed with *keep* (*on*), as in *I keep* (*on*) *losing my keys* and *I kept* (*on*) *failing my driving test.*

JK

jocular formation A word which is constructed purely as a joke and, as a rule, does not gain a place in the language. Examples include *wasm* ('an outdated doctrine', based on *ism*) and *monokini* ('bikini with no top', from *bikini* with replacement of the accidental syllable *bi-*, resembling the prefix *bi-* 'two', by *mono-* 'one').

jussive A traditional label for a verb-form or a sentence structure which expresses some kind of command. The jussive includes the ordinary IMPERATIVE, as in *Wash your hands!* But it also includes other structures, such as *Everybody pay attention* and *Let's go*. Sometimes the label is applied more narrowly to a command directed at someone other than the addressee, as in *Let them eat cake!*, when this is interpreted as an instruction to 'them', and not as an order to the addressee.

L

labile verb A verb which can be either TRANSITIVE or INTRANSITIVE, with related meanings. English has many of these, divided into a number of subclasses. Examples: *Susie smokes Turkish cigarettes*; *Susie smokes*; *Susie undressed the children*; *Susie undressed*; *The sub sank the ship*; *The ship sank*; *Susie washed her bikini*; *This bikini washes easily*; *She swam the Channel*; *She swam slowly*; *Susie jumped the horse over the fence*; *The horse jumped over the fence*; *They are reprinting my book*; *My book is reprinting*.

learnèd word A word taken from a classical language. For example, instead of *breakable*, English often uses the Latin word *fragile*; instead of *dog*, we sometimes use the Latin word *canine*; instead of saying that a disease is *catching*, we often prefer the Latin word *infectious*.

left-branching Any grammatical construction in which elements are added to the left-hand end of something which is already present. Typical of some languages, such as Japanese and Basque, left-branching is unusual in English, but it does occur in the SAXON GENITIVE: *my mother's sister's neighbour's doctor's husband*. Compare RIGHT-BRANCHING.

left-dislocation See under DISLOCATION.

lemma A formal term for HEADWORD, preferred by the writers of dictionaries.

lexeme Another term for LEXICAL ITEM.

lexical Pertaining to words.

lexical ambiguity An AMBIGUITY which resides within a single word. An example is *port* in *The sailors enjoyed the port.* Here *port* can mean either 'city by the sea' or 'fortified wine'. Compare STRUCTURAL AMBIGUITY.

lexical category Another term for PART OF SPEECH.

lexical entry In an idealized formal grammar of a language, the information required to describe the behaviour of a single LEXICAL ITEM (word). For each lexical item, its lexical entry provides its part of speech, its pronunciation, its meaning, and all unpredictable or irregular details of its grammatical behaviour.

lexical item (also **lexeme**) A WORD considered as an item of vocabulary, apart from any variation in form it may exhibit for grammatical purposes. A lexical item is a word in the sense in which a dictionary lists words. For example, *dog* is a lexical item of English with the two grammatical forms *dog* and *dogs*, and *take* is a lexical item with the grammatical forms *take, takes, took, taking* and *taken*. Compare WORD-FORM.

lexical morpheme A MORPHEME which has dictionary meaning. Examples: *woman, green, decide, under,* the *bio-* of *biology* and the *step-* of *stepmother*. Compare GRAMMATICAL MORPHEME.

lexicalization The expression of a meaning by a single word. For example, in English, 'adult male equine' is lexicalized as *stallion*, 'adult female equine' as *mare*, and 'equine' as *horse*. However, while 'adult male bovine' is lexicalized as *bull* and 'adult female bovine' as *cow*, there is no lexicalization for 'bovine': we have no word to denote any bovine animal, parallel to *horse* for equine animals.

lexical verb (also **main verb**) Any VERB which is not an AUXILIARY. For example, in the sentence *I must have tried fifteen bookshops*, the lexical verb is *try*, while *must* and *have* are auxiliaries. Among the thousands of lexical verbs in English are *run, smile, die, elope, describe, explain, kill, tickle, grow* and *analyse*.

lexicography The writing of dictionaries. A writer of dictionaries is a *lexicographer*.

lexicon (also **lexis**) The set of words in a language, sometimes particularly together with their LEXICAL ENTRIES and with the rules for constructing words from other words. It is most usual to apply VOCABULARY to the words known by a person but *lexicon* to the words in a language.

light verb A VERB which has no meaning of its own but which serves merely to convert another word into a verbal form. The English verbs which can serve as light verbs are *do, make, have, give* and *take*. Examples of expressions involving a light verb: *do a dance, make a move, have a smoke, give a shrug* and *take a sip*. A sentence with a light verb often expresses a subtle nuance of meaning: for example, *Susie took a sip of her drink* does not mean quite the same as *Susie sipped her drink*. But note that these verbs can also serve as ordinary (not light) verbs, as with *make* in *Susie made a coffee table* and *give* in *Susie gave Natalie a present*.

linking verb Another term for COPULA or QUASI-COPULA.

loan shift A shift in the meaning of a word to accommodate a new concept acquired from speakers of another language. For example, in pagan England, *hell* meant 'pagan underworld' and *heaven* meant only 'sky', but the introduction of Christianity from abroad caused these words to lose their original meanings in favour of new Christian concepts.

loan-translation Another term for CALQUE.

loanword A word which is taken over by BORROWING; see that entry.

locative A word or form expressing location. English most commonly does this by using one of the prepositions *in, on* and *at*: *in the bedroom, on the table, at the pub*.

logogram (also **symbol**) A character which conventionally represents a word or a phrase without using the letters of the alphabet. Familiar examples include the symbols 5 for *five*, $ for *dollars*, @ for *at* and § for *section*. A logogram differs from a PICTOGRAM in that a pictogram is clearly meant to be a picture of what it represents while a logogram is not: a logogram is entirely arbitrary in form. Like a pictogram, a logogram is *not* an ABBREVIATION.

In a purely logographic writing system, such as that of Chinese, all words are written with logograms, and the total number of symbols required runs into the thousands. In the alphabetic English writing system, we don't strictly require any logograms at all, but we find the use of logograms convenient as a brief way of writing things that are either very frequent or rather long: most people prefer to write *£487*, with logograms, rather than to write out *four hundred and eighty-seven pounds*.

long passive See under PASSIVE VOICE.

M

main clause A CLAUSE which is capable of making a complete sentence by itself; a clause which is not a SUBORDINATE CLAUSE. A sentence always contains at least one main clause, and a SIMPLE SENTENCE consists only of a single main clause. In the simple sentence *Susie finished her drink*, the whole sentence is the main clause. In the COMPOUND SENTENCE *Susie cooked dinner, and Natalie did the washing-up*, there are two main clauses connected by *and*. See also MATRIX CLAUSE.

main verb Another term for LEXICAL VERB.

major lexical category (also **major part of speech**) A label for any PART OF SPEECH seen as especially important. Traditionally, the major classes were the four OPEN CLASSES of English: noun, verb, adjective, adverb. In much contemporary theorizing, however, the major classes are taken to be noun, verb, adjective and preposition.

malapropism (also **catachresis**) The use of the wrong word, often especially when another word of similar sound is intended. Examples: *He lay prostate on the floor* (intended *prostrate*); *The All Blacks scored a fortuitous try* (intended *fortunate*); *We have a mutual interest in this* (intended *common interest*).

manner adverb An ADVERB that answers the question 'how?' Examples: *slowly, carefully, rashly, enthusiastically, grudgingly*. An ADVERBIAL PHRASE that does the same is a *manner adverbial*: *with a sly expression, in hope, without hesitation*.

marked form See under MARKEDNESS.

markedness A difference in the status of two forms or constructions which exist side by side in a language but which exhibit a difference in complexity or applicability. One of these, the UNMARKED FORM, is the 'ordinary' or 'basic' form, while the other, the MARKED FORM, differs from the first in containing extra material or in being confined to special contexts.

For example, *cat* is unmarked, while its plural *cats* is marked by the suffix *-s*. Likewise, *lion* is unmarked, while the female *lioness* is marked by the suffix *-ess*, and *consistent* is unmarked in comparison with its negative *inconsistent*. The active sentence *The police arrested Susie* is unmarked with respect to its passive counterpart *Susie was arrested by the police*, which contains more material. Of the two plurals of *brother*, *brothers* is unmarked (used in most contexts), while *brethren* is marked (used only in certain religious contexts).

masculine In some languages with GENDER, a gender class which shows some degree of correlation with male sex. Many European languages have such a gender class, but the correlation with male sex is usually rather weak. In French, for example, most nouns denoting males are grammatically masculine, but there are exceptions, such as *sentinelle* 'sentry', which is grammatically feminine, even though most sentries are men. In any case, most masculine nouns in French denote things which have no sex at all, such as *livre* 'book' and *argent* 'money'.

mass noun (also **non-count noun**, **uncountable noun**) A NOUN which denotes something which cannot be counted, such as *wheat*, *sand* or *wine*. A mass noun cannot normally be counted or pluralized: **these wheats*, **two sands*. An exception occurs with SECONDARY RECATEGORIZATION: *these wines*.

matrix clause A clause which contains a SUBORDINATE CLAUSE within it. In the COMPLEX SENTENCE *The employees who were dismissed are suing the company*, the matrix clause is *The employees . . . are suing the company*, while the remainder is the subordinate clause (a RELATIVE CLAUSE) contained within it.

Does the subordinate clause itself form part of its matrix clause? Traditional grammarians usually answered 'no' to this question, but contemporary linguists more often prefer to answer 'yes'.

A matrix clause is often a MAIN CLAUSE, as in the example above, but it need not be: it can itself be a subordinate clause. In the sentence *The victim told police that the man who attacked her had had a beard,* the subordinate clause *who attacked her* is contained within the subordinate clause *that the man . . . had had a beard.*

mediopassive The construction in which an intrinsically TRANSITIVE verb is construed intransitively with a patient as its subject and receives a PASSIVE interpretation, even though the construction is not formally passive. Examples: *This fabric washes easily*; *My new book is selling well.* In these examples, somebody unspecified is washing the fabric and selling the book. In the past, only a few English verbs could appear in this construction, but, in contemporary English, most speakers are happy to accept many more verbs in it: *This wall will paint* (*up*) *pretty well*; *That carpet should hoover without much difficulty*; *This grass will cut easily enough.* Note that the mediopassive construction is usually only possible with an adverb phrase expressing ease or difficulty. A verb which can appear in the mediopassive is one kind of LABILE VERB. Note: the mediopassive has sometimes been called the MIDDLE, but this name is not recommended.

metalanguage A language used to talk about a language. For example, terms like *noun, transitive verb, relative clause* and *prepositional phrase* constitute part of the metalanguage we use for talking about English grammar.

metanalysis The process in which a sound is transferred from the end of one word to the beginning of the next word, or vice-versa. For example, the earlier *an ewt* has become *a newt,* while the earlier *a numpire* has become *an umpire.*

metaphor The use, for effect, of words which are not literally accurate but which call up a resemblance. For example, we may speak of a failing business as *a lame duck,* meaning that, like a lamed creature, it is unable to compete effectively with healthy competitors. A great deal of the grammar of any language is metaphorical in origin. For example, we say *in the morning,* as though a morning were a location.

middle A label which has been applied by grammarians to a very wide range of different things. Most commonly, perhaps, this term is used to mean either MEDIOPASSIVE or RELATIONAL VERB, though it has also been used in other senses.

minor lexical category (also **minor part of speech**) Any PART OF SPEECH which is not a MAJOR LEXICAL CATEGORY; see that entry.

minor sentence Any piece of speech or writing which does not have the form of a complete sentence but which is normal in context. Examples: *Why not do it now?*; *Any news?*; *All aboard!*; *No smoking*; *This way, please*; *As if I would know*.

modal (also **modal auxiliary**) Any one of the several English AUXILIARY verbs which serve to express aspects of MODALITY and which exhibit rather distinctive grammatical behaviour. The English modals are *may, might, can, could, will, would, shall, should, must* and the somewhat anomalous *ought*; the two verbs *dare* and *need* sometimes also behave like modals, and are then called SEMI-MODALS. Like other auxiliaries, the modals exhibit the NICE PROPERTIES; unlike the PRIMARY AUXILIARIES, however, the modals have only finite (tensed) forms, with no participles, gerunds or infinitives, and they also fail to take *-s* in the third-person singular: *She can do it*, not **She cans do it*.

modality A label for those aspects of meaning centring on possibility, probability, certainty, impossibility, permission, obligation and prohibition. In English, these notions are most commonly expressed by means of our MODAL auxiliaries, sometimes combined with *not*.

modifier Any word or phrase which limits the meaning of another word, usually the HEAD of the phrase containing both. For example, given the phrase *the dog*, we can introduce various modifiers to narrow its applicability: *the big dog, the new dog, the dog on the left, the dog I got for Christmas*, and so on. See PREMODIFIER and POSTMODIFIER for more examples, and compare SPECIFIER.

mood The GRAMMATICAL CATEGORY which correlates with the degree or kind of reality assigned by the speaker to what she is saying. Traditional grammarians recognize four or five moods: INDICATIVE (utterance presented as a fact), SUBJUNCTIVE (utterance presented as doubtful or unreal), IMPERATIVE (utterance presented as a command), OPTATIVE (utterance presented as a wish) and sometimes INTERROGATIVE (utterance presented as a question). This is because, in the classical languages

Latin and Greek, all but the interrogative are marked by distinctive verb-forms.

In English, however, we generally lack distinctive verb-forms for distinguishing moods, and the distinctions, where they are made at all, are made almost entirely by the use of different sentence structures:

Indicative: *Susie is being hired.*
Subjunctive: [*I suggest*] *that Susie* (*should*) *be hired.*
Imperative: *Hire Susie!*
Optative: *May Susie be hired.*
Interrogative: *Is Susie going to be hired?*

Only the subjunctive is very occasionally marked by distinct verb-forms; see SUBJUNCTIVE for details. All further distinctions of mood are made in English by adding words: *Susie will probably be hired; Maybe Susie will be hired; Surely Susie will be hired; I doubt that Susie will be hired.* Consequently, modern grammarians, instead of speaking of mood in English, often prefer to speak of (formal) SENTENCE TYPES.

morph **1**. Another term for ALLOMORPH; see under MORPHEME.

2. Any piece of a word we may want to talk about, sometimes including the whole word. We might speak of the *cran-* of *cranberry* as a morph, or the *-o-* of *kissogram*, or the entire word *took*.

morpheme The minimal unit of word structure. For example, *cat* consists of a single morpheme {cat}, *doghouse* consists of the two morphemes {dog} and {house}, *happiness* consists of the two morphemes {happy} and {-ness}, *rewrite* consists of the two morphemes {re-} and {write}, and *recrystallized* consists of the four morphemes {re-}, {crystal}, {-ize} and {-ed}. A particular morpheme may appear in more than one shape, depending on context; these variant forms are the morpheme's ALLOMORPHS (or MORPHS). For example, the morpheme {sane} has one allomorph in *sane* and *insane*, but a different one in *sanity* (listen to the pronunciations), and the negative prefix {in-} has several allomorphs in *insane, impossible* and *illegal*. See PORTMANTEAU MORPH, EMPTY MORPH.

morphology Word structure, or the study of word structure. Morphology is divided into two main areas: INFLECTIONAL MORPHOLOGY (the way in which words vary their shapes for grammatical purposes) and WORD-FORMATION (the construction of new words from the resources of the language). See these entries.

morphosyntax The link between MORPHOLOGY (word-form) and SYNTAX (sentence structure). For example, the English pronoun *he* must appear in the form *him* in certain syntactic positions: *We saw him*; *We gave it to him*. This is a morphosyntactic observation.

N

natural gender An inappropriate label sometimes applied to English, which has no grammatical GENDER. English has a certain amount of sex-marking, as in *he* versus *she* and *duke* versus *duchess*. But sex is a matter of biology, while gender is a matter of grammar, and it is an error to confuse the biological sex-marking of English with the gender distinctions found in some other languages.

negation The use of a NEGATIVE element, especially of *not* or of a NEGATIVE AUXILIARY like *can't*.

negative An element which reverses the truth value of a statement, changing it from true to false or vice versa. The most familiar English negative is *not*: the truth value of *Susie will be there* is reversed in its negation *Susie will not be there*. Often *not* combines with an auxiliary to produce a NEGATIVE AUXILIARY. Several pronouns, adverbs and determiners also have negative senses: the pronouns *nobody, no one, nothing* and *none*, the adverbs *nowhere* and *never*, and the determiner *no*, as in *We have no wine*.

See also SEMI-NEGATIVE.

negative auxiliary The distinctive and sometimes irregularly constructed negated forms of the English AUXILIARIES, such as *don't, doesn't, can't, won't* and *mustn't*.

negative concord The technical term for a DOUBLE NEGATIVE.

negative polarity item An item which can only occur in certain contexts, notably negative sentences and questions. A good example is *any*: it is normal to say *We don't have any wine* and *Do we have any wine?*, but it is impossible to say **We have any wine*. Other examples are *ever* and *anything*.

negative raising The construction in which a negative element appears earlier in a sentence than is logically appropriate. For example, the common construction *I can't seem to find my keys* exhibits negative raising from *I seem unable to find my keys*.

neologism A word which has been recently coined. Some fairly recent English examples are *eco-friendly* 'not harmful to the environment' and *geopathic* 'pertaining to illnesses caused by radioactive rocks'.

neuter In some GENDER languages, a conventional label for a gender class exhibiting no correlation with sex.

new See under GIVEN AND NEW.

NICE properties A mnemonic for the four properties which distinguish AUXILIARY verbs from other verbs, as follows.

1. Auxiliaries alone can be negated: *She doesn't smoke; She wouldn't smoke; She's not smoking*; but not **She smokes not.*

2. Auxiliaries alone can be inverted: *Is she smoking?; Does she smoke?; May she smoke?*; but not **Smokes she?*

3. Auxiliaries alone exhibit *code*, the ability to allow a following verb phrase to be deleted: *Will she take the job? I think she should, and she probably will, but Mike thinks she can't.*

4. Auxiliaries alone can be emphasized: *She DOES smoke; She MUSTN'T smoke; She CAN smoke; She IS smoking.*

nominal group A syntactic unit which can combine with a DETERMINER to make a NOUN PHRASE. A typical nominal group can fill the blank in the following frame to make a good sentence: *The __ was/were nice*. Examples: *young lady, rest of the meal, other people, meal I had last night, puppies*. Linguists often apply the term *N-bar* to this category. Note that a few linguists use this term in a completely different way, sometimes as a synonym for noun phrase, but these other uses are not standard.

nominalization Any word or construction in which a linguistic unit belonging to another category is converted to a noun-like category. For example, the verb *arrive* can be nominalized into the noun *arrival*, and the adjective *absent* can be nominalized into the noun *absence*. But more complex examples exist. In *That she smokes surprises me*, the NOUN PHRASE *that she smokes* is a nominalization of the sentence *she smokes*; in *Lisa's going topless upset her father*, the noun phrase *Lisa's going topless* is a nominalization of the sentence *Lisa went topless*; and in *To quit your job would be a mistake*, the noun phrase *to quit your job* is a nominalization of the VERB PHRASE *quit your job*. A GERUND represents another kind of nominalization.

nominative In many languages with CASE, the case-form used to mark a grammatical SUBJECT, and sometimes for other purposes. In English, only a few pronouns distinguish case. For example, the first-person singular pronoun has nominative *I*, as in *I saw her*, as opposed to the OBJECTIVE form *me*, as in *She saw me*.

nominative absolute Another name for ABSOLUTE CONSTRUCTION.

nonce form A form which is created on a particular occasion and which does not find a lasting place in the language. Two examples are *disclude*, heard as the opposite of *include*, and *techno-anorak* for 'computer addict'.

non-count noun Another term for MASS NOUN.

non-defining Another term for NON-RESTRICTIVE; see under RESTRICTIVE.

non-finite A label applied to a verb-form which is not marked for TENSE and which cannot be the only verb in a clause. A typical English verb usually has the following non-finite forms: the PRESENT PARTICIPLE (ending in *-ing*), the PAST PARTICIPLE (usually ending in *-ed* or in *-en*), the INFINITIVE (with no ending), and the GERUND (also ending in *-ing*).

It is not always easy to distinguish non-finite forms from FINITE ones in English, because some finite forms carry no marking and are therefore identical to the infinitive. For example, in *I leave for work at 8.30*, the verb-form *leave* is finite, while in *I decided to leave for work*, *leave* is non-finite (it is an infinitive).

non-past Another name for the PRESENT tense in English.

non-restrictive See under RESTRICTIVE.

notional definition A definition based on meaning. TRADITIONAL GRAMMAR made heavy use of notional definitions, but these don't really work. The categories we work with in grammar are defined by their shared grammatical properties, not by their meanings. For example, the grammarians of the past often defined a NOUN as 'the name of a person, place or thing'. Well, *red* is certainly the name of a colour, and so by this definition it ought to be a noun – yet it is most commonly an adjective, as in *a red skirt*. In fact, nouns like *arrival* and *absence* are really no more the names of anything than is the verb *arrive* or the adjective *absent*: these words are nouns because they behave grammatically like nouns, and not because they are the names of something 'out there'.

noun The PART OF SPEECH which includes words like *dog, tree, niece, arrival, pursuit* and *number*. The easiest way to identify nouns is to consider the following frames: *The* __ *was nice*; *The* __ *were nice*. Any single word which can fill one of the blanks to produce a grammatical sentence (though not necessarily a sensible one) is a noun, because the grammar of English permits nouns, and only nouns, to fill such positions. So, for example, *spinach, girls, entertainment, kangaroo, police* and *torture* can fit into one of the blanks, and hence these words can be nouns in English – though the last one can also be a VERB. But the words *happy, with, slowly, admire* and *this* cannot fill either of the blanks, and so these words cannot be nouns.

The reason we needed two frames above is that English nouns distinguish NUMBER: that is, most nouns can be either SINGULAR or PLURAL. This is the only kind of INFLECTION exhibited by nouns in English; see NUMBER for discussion. In some other languages, nouns exhibit one or both of GENDER and CASE.

In the great majority of instances, the HEAD of a NOUN PHRASE is a noun.

noun clause A traditional label for any kind of SUBORDINATE CLAUSE which appears to occupy the position of a NOUN PHRASE. This label includes several rather different cases, as follows:

1. A VERB-COMPLEMENT CLAUSE: *Susie has decided that she will quit her job* (see under COMPLEMENT CLAUSE).

2. A SENTENTIAL SUBJECT: *That she is not here worries me.*
3. An EMBEDDED QUESTION: *I don't know what we should do.*
4. A FREE RELATIVE: *I want to find whoever did this.*

In most contemporary work, we avoid the term *noun clause* in favour of the more specific labels.

noun-complement clause See under COMPLEMENT CLAUSE.

noun phrase (NP) A syntactic unit which can serve as any GRAMMATICAL RELATION in a sentence, such as SUBJECT, DIRECT OBJECT or object of a PREPOSITION. A noun phrase may be of any size or degree of complexity, from one word to dozens of words. Here is a simple test. Any phrase which can fit into one of the following blanks to make a grammatical sentence is a noun phrase: __ *was nice*; __ *were nice*. So, all of the following are noun phrases: *she, Susie, the party, your sister's boyfriend, the women we met at Mike's party the other night, none of the people on the interview panel*.

A noun phrase is constructed around a NOUN or a PRONOUN as its HEAD. In my examples, the heads are *she, Susie, party, boyfriend, women* and *none*.

noun used as adjective An old-fashioned label for a NOUN used to modify another noun, such as the first noun in *bus station, pea soup* or *physics textbook*. The term is inaccurate and should not be used, since a noun in this position remains a noun and does not become an adjective.

NP The abbreviation for NOUN PHRASE.

null anaphor See under ANAPHOR.

number The GRAMMATICAL CATEGORY which relates to the number of countable objects in the world. In English, number is mainly important with NOUNS. An English noun usually exhibits a two-way distinction of number: a SINGULAR form, denoting one of something, and a PLURAL form, denoting two or more. As a rule, the singular form has no particular marking, while the plural form carries the suffix *-s* or *-es*. Example: *dog/dogs*; *box/boxes*; *amusement/amusements*. But a few dozen nouns form their plurals irregularly. Examples: *child/children*; *man/men*; *woman/women*; *tooth/teeth*; *mouse/mice*; *sheep/sheep*; *radius/*

radii; *phenomenon/phenomena*; *bacterium/bacteria*. (Note that *sheep* really does have singular and plural forms, even though these are identical: *This sheep is hungry*; *These sheep are hungry*.)

Some nouns are unusual in having only a singular form or only a plural form. Nouns which have only a singular form include *furniture*, *wheat*, *happiness*, *gratitude*, *knitting* and *rugby*. Nouns which have only a plural form include *police*, *cattle*, *oats*, *tweezers*, *pants*, *pliers* and *remains*; see PLURALE TANTUM. Still other nouns normally have only a singular form, and can be pluralized only in special senses; see SECONDARY RECATEGORIZATION.

An English noun must always appear either in a singular form or in a plural form. There is no possibility of avoiding the choice, even when it appears irrelevant. For example, it is far from clear that the distinction between one object and more than one is of any relevance to grain, but the grammar of English forces us to choose one form or the other, and so we make arbitrary choices: *wheat* is singular (and has no plural), while *oats* is plural (and has no singular).

numeral See CARDINAL NUMERAL, ORDINAL NUMERAL.

O

object Any of several different GRAMMATICAL RELATIONS. See DIRECT OBJECT, INDIRECT OBJECT, OBLIQUE OBJECT.

object control See under CONTROL.

objective In English, the CASE form used with certain pronouns to mark a non-subject. Only the following pronouns distinguish a NOMINATIVE form (the subject form) from an objective form: *I* (nominative)/*me* (objective); *he/him*; *she/her*; *we/us*; *they/them*; and, very marginally, *who/whom*. Other pronouns, like *you*, *it* and *what*, are invariable in form. The objective is sometimes called the ACCUSATIVE, but this name is not really appropriate.

objective genitive A POSSESSIVE phrase with *of* or *-'s* in which the thing possessed is interpreted as a logical object. For example, *the destruction of the city* is logically related to *destroyed the city*, and *the manager's dismissal* is in most cases related to *dismissed the manager*. Compare SUBJECTIVE GENITIVE.

object of comparison In English, the object of the preposition *than*, such as *China* in *India is growing faster than China* and *me* in *Susie is taller than me*. In English, there is little difference between an object of comparison and any other object of a preposition, though the same is not true of all languages.

object of preposition See OBLIQUE OBJECT.

object raising The construction in which the logical object of a subordinate clause appears as the surface subject of a main clause. For example, *To please Susie is hard* is more idiomatically expressed as *Susie* *is hard to please*. Here *Susie*, the logical object of *please*, appears as the surface subject of *is*.

oblique object (also **object of a preposition**) In English, the NOUN PHRASE which follows a PREPOSITION. Examples (in brackets): *before* [*the war*]; *in* [*the shower*]; *a bottle* [*of wine*]; *without* [*any assistance*]; *under* [*the bed*].

open class A PART OF SPEECH which is large and which accepts new members easily. In English, the open classes are NOUN, VERB, ADJECTIVE and ADVERB.

optative The MOOD category which expresses a wish. The only distinctive optative constructions in English are rather archaic: *Would that we were at home*; *May you be happy always*.

ordinal numeral Any number term of the form *first, second, third, fourth, fifth, twenty-seventh* or *three hundredth*. The English ordinals are usually classed as ADJECTIVES. Compare CARDINAL NUMERAL.

orthographic word Anything which is conventionally written with a white space at each end but no white space in the middle. For example, *dog, girl's, land-owners* and *thermonuclear* are all single orthographic words, while *ice cream, New Zealand* and *cocktail dress* are not, even though each of the last three is arguably a single word in some important sense – for example, each would receive an entry in the dictionary.

orthography A conventional way of writing a language, or the rules governing this. Most obviously, the orthography of English includes the conventions for spelling words, but the use of capital letters and of punctuation is also part of the orthography. For example, English orthography requires *precede* and *proceed*, while the spellings *preceed* and *procede* are not acceptable, and it requires the possessive to be spelled *its* and not *it's*.

P

paradigm A list of the set of forms which can be assumed by a word for grammatical purposes. English has very little in the way of paradigms, but some other languages have far more. An example is Latin, one of whose paradigms is this: *amo* 'I love', *amas* 'you (singular) love', *amat* 's/he loves', *amamus* 'we love', *amatis* 'you (plural) love', *amant* 'they love'. Note how the Latin forms vary constantly, while the English paradigm distinguishes only *loves* from all the others.

paradigmatic relation The relation which holds among a set of linguistic items or forms which have the property that only one of them is present in a given case. For example, *I* and *me* are in a paradigmatic relation: in any circumstance in which one of them is required, the rules of English grammar require either one or the other to be present. Examples: *I did it*; *I'm American*; *She saw me*; *Can anybody lend me a fiver?* Compare SYNTAGMATIC RELATION.

paraphrase Either of two structurally different sentences which are related in meaning in the following way: if one of them is true, then the other must be true. Examples: *Susie bought a car from Mike/Mike sold a car to Susie*; *The Mongols sacked Kiev/Kiev was sacked by the Mongols*; *Susie is older than Natalie/Natalie is younger than Susie.*

Paraphrase is a useful way of distinguishing the meanings of an ambiguous sentence. For example, the two meanings of the ambiguous string *The target was not hit by many arrows* can be revealed by offering a paraphrase of each: *Few arrows hit the target* for one, and *Many arrows missed the target* for the other.

parataxis Juxtaposing two or more CLAUSES without the use of SUBORDINATION (or HYPOTAXIS). Example: *It was the best of times; it was the worst of times*. Some, but not all, authorities apply this term to cases in which the clauses are connected by *and* or a similar word: *It was the best of times, and it was the worst of times*. Note the difference in the following examples. Paratactic: *John and Esther got married, and then they bought a house*. Hypotactic: *After they got married, John and Esther bought a house*.

parenthetical An interruption, in the middle of a sentence, which is not grammatically connected to the rest of its sentence. In writing, a parenthetical is set off by a pair of dashes, by a pair of parentheses, or (if not too strong) by a pair of commas. The sequences set off in the following examples are parentheticals: *The destruction of Guernica – and there is no doubt the destruction was deliberate – horrified the world; Otto Jespersen (1860–1943) was one of the greatest linguists of the twentieth century; Bill Clinton, as they say in Arkansas, was a hard dog to keep on the porch*.

parse To analyse the grammatical structure of (a sentence). Parsing sentences was once a familiar classroom exercise in the teaching of English grammar in schools. Today this is no longer usual, but university students of linguistics and of English language are still expected to learn parsing, and so, in some traditions, are the learners of foreign languages.

participial adjective A word-form which is identical in form to the (present or past) PARTICIPLE of a verb but which functions as an ADJECTIVE. Examples (in brackets): *[missing] persons, a [smiling] face, a [loving] family, a [surprising] result, an [expected] visitor, a [delayed] appearance, a [vanished] civilization, [determined] investigators*.

participial relative clause (also **reduced relative clause**) A construction which resembles a RELATIVE CLAUSE but which contains a PARTICIPLE instead of a finite verb. In the following examples, the first member of the pair contains a participial relative clause, while the second contains an equivalent full relative clause. *The employees sacked by the company are going to court; The employees who were sacked by the company are going to court; The woman playing the flute is my wife; The woman who is playing the flute is my wife*.

participle A NON-FINITE form of a VERB with certain special functions. English has two participles: the PRESENT PARTICIPLE and the PAST PARTICIPLE; see these entries for more information.

particle **1**. Broadly, any grammatical word of invariable form, such as *of, and, the, to* or *up*.

2. Narrowly, a small word making up the second part of a PHRASAL VERB, such as the *up* of *make up*.

partitive A form meaning 'some of'. English usually expresses this with *of*, as in *some of the men* and *most of the men*. Some other languages have a distinct form for this.

part of speech (also **word class**, **lexical category**) Any one of the several classes into which the lexical items (words) of a language are divided on the basis of their grammatical behaviour. Languages differ in the parts of speech they possess. For English, this dictionary recognizes the following twelve parts of speech: NOUN, VERB, ADJECTIVE, ADVERB, PRONOUN, PREPOSITION, CONJUNCTION, DETERMINER, DEGREE MODIFIER, COMPLEMENTIZER, SUBORDINATOR, and the rather marginal INTERJECTION. A few grammarians regard AUXILIARY as a class distinct from *verb* and QUANTIFIER as a class distinct from *determiner*, but these further classes are not usual.

Words are assigned to parts of speech according to their grammatical behaviour. Most especially, we classify words according to their DISTRIBUTION (the positions in which they can occur), their INFLECTION (the way they change their forms for grammatical reasons), and their possibilities for DERIVATION (sense 1) (their ability to accept prefixes and suffixes in order to form other words). Unlike earlier grammarians, we do not try to classify words according to their meanings, since the meaning of a word is not at all a reliable guide to its grammatical behaviour.

Words are placed together in a single part of speech because they have important grammatical properties in common, but not all the words in a single part of speech necessarily have grammatical properties which are entirely identical: see SUBCATEGORIZATION.

In English, a single word must often be assigned to two or more parts of speech. For example, *kiss* is a noun in *Give me a kiss* but a verb in *Kiss me*, and *straight* is an adjective in *a straight line*, an adverb in *He can't walk straight*, and a noun in *Schumacher accelerated down the straight*.

A few words exhibit unique behaviour and cannot sensibly be assigned to any part of speech at all. English examples include the negative *not*, the polite *please* and the infinitival *to*, all of these being illustrated by the example *Please do not try to stand up*.

Desk dictionaries of English, though they have improved greatly in recent years, are still often rather old-fashioned and outdated in their part-of-speech labels. You should be a little careful about accepting dictionary labels at face value.

passive voice The construction in which the logical object of a verb becomes its grammatical subject, while its logical subject is either reduced to a PREPOSITIONAL PHRASE introduced by *by* or removed from the sentence altogether.

Consider the sentence *Madame Curie discovered radium in 1898*, which is in the ACTIVE VOICE. Here the logical subject *Madame Curie* is also the grammatical subject. This has two corresponding passive forms. The LONG PASSIVE, or passive with agent, is this: *Radium was discovered in 1898 by Madame Curie*, or, equally, *Radium was discovered by Madame Curie in 1898*. In this case, the logical subject appears after *by*. The SHORT PASSIVE, or AGENTLESS PASSIVE, is this: *Radium was discovered in 1898*. Here the logical subject is omitted.

In English, the passive voice is constructed by combining either the verb *be* or the verb *get* with the PAST PARTICIPLE of the lexical verb. As a rule, only the passive with *be* is found in formal English, and the passive with *get* (the *GET*-PASSIVE) is strictly informal. Compare the *be*-passive *England were beaten by Australia* with the *get*-passive *England got beat by Australia*.

As a rule, any TRANSITIVE verb can appear in the passive voice, but there are a few exceptions, like *have, fit* and *weigh*: *Susie has blue eyes*, but not **Blue eyes are had by Susie*; *That dress fits you*, but not **You are fitted by that dress*; *Susie weighs nine stone*, but not **Nine stone is weighed by Susie*. An INTRANSITIVE verb cannot normally appear in the passive at all, but see PREPOSITIONAL PASSIVE for an exception.

A construction formally identical to the passive occurs in English with the distinctive class of verbs called PSYCH-VERBS. Note also that a STATIVE construction often looks just like a passive in form, even though it is not passive.

passive participle Another name for the English PAST PARTICIPLE, when this is used in the PASSIVE VOICE.

past (also **preterite**) The usual name for a TENSE category which most typically refers to a time before the moment of speaking. English has only two tenses, the past and the PRESENT. With most English verbs, the past tense is marked by the suffix *-ed*, though a number of verbs have an irregular past tense. A past-tense form in English can be identified by its ability to co-occur with an adverb of past time, such as *yesterday*. Examples: (regular) *I washed the car yesterday*; *It rained yesterday*; *They delivered our furniture yesterday*; (irregular) *I saw Susie yesterday*; *I bought a car yesterday*; *We took the dog to the vet yesterday*; *I had a bad experience yesterday*; *I was busy yesterday*.

The forms illustrated above are examples of the SIMPLE PAST, in which no AUXILIARY is present. The simple past exhibits PERFECTIVE aspect. But it is possible to combine a past-tense form of the auxiliary *be* with a PRESENT PARTICIPLE in order to construct the past continuous: *Susie was smoking a cigarette*; *We were watching the cricket*. It is also possible to combine a past-tense form of the auxiliary *have* with a PAST PARTICIPLE in order to construct the PAST PERFECT: *Susie had finished her dinner*; *We had drunk the wine*.

English also has a special past-tense form to express HABITUAL aspect in the past: the *used to* construction, as in *I used to live in Liverpool*; *Susie used to smoke*.

The past tense does not always refer to past time. Consider the example *It's time you went to bed*. Here the past-tense form *went* refers to the immediate future, not to the past. And consider the example *If I spoke better French, I could get a job in Paris*. Here the past-tense form *spoke* refers to a hypothetical present, not to the past. This is an example of a COUNTERFACTUAL; see under CONDITIONAL SENTENCE.

past anterior A construction which indicates that one event preceded another in the past. English can express this either with the simple past or with the PAST PERFECT. For example, to show that I ate dinner and that Susie arrived (in that order) in the past, I can say either *I ate dinner before Susie arrived* or *I had eaten dinner before Susie arrived*.

past participle (also **perfect participle**) A particular NON-FINITE form of an English VERB. With a REGULAR verb, this form ends in *-ed* and is identical in form to the PAST tense: *loved, waited, decided*. With an IRREGULAR verb, it has any of a variety of forms, though it often ends in *-en*: *broken, written, spoken, seen, drawn, sat, put*. The past participle has several uses.

First, it combines with the AUXILIARY *have* to make the PERFECT forms of verbs: *I have seen her; I had finished dinner*. Second, it can be used as an ADJECTIVE: *boiled cabbage, dried tomatoes, a vanished civilization*. (Note: a few verbs use for this purpose a different form of the past participle from the ordinary one: *The metal has melted*, but *molten metal; I have mowed the grass*, but *new-mown hay*.) Third, it can be used in a PARTICIPIAL RELATIVE CLAUSE: *The fossils discovered by the Leakey family have revolutionized our understanding of human evolution*. Fourth, it can be used to construct the PASSIVE VOICE: *Fred Lieb was invited to write his autobiography*. In this last function, the participle is sometimes called the PASSIVE PARTICIPLE.

Compare PRESENT PARTICIPLE.

past perfect (also **pluperfect**) The English construction in which *had* is combined with the PAST PARTICIPLE of a verb. This is the past-tense form corresponding to the PRESENT PERFECT, and it often has a comparable meaning to the present perfect: it presents a state of affairs in the past resulting from an earlier event. For example, *I had finished the wine* commonly means 'There was no wine at the (past) time I am talking about, because I drank the last of it earlier.' However, the past perfect can also be used as a PAST ANTERIOR; see this entry.

The past perfect can also be used to express an unreal condition in the past. Example: *If the Germans had invaded the USSR in April, they might have captured Moscow*. Here the use of the past perfect *had invaded* indicates that the Germans did not in fact invade in April. This is an example of a COUNTERFACTUAL; see under CONDITIONAL SENTENCE.

patient The SEMANTIC ROLE borne by the entity which is directly affected by the action of the verb. In a TRANSITIVE sentence, a patient, if present, is usually the DIRECT OBJECT. In the following examples, the objects are patients: *Susie slapped Mike; Susie is repainting the bedroom; Susie stroked the cat; Susie is washing the car*. (But note that not all direct objects are patients: the objects are not patients in *Susie received a letter* or *Susie loves Natalie*.) In an INTRANSITIVE sentence, it is possible for the SUBJECT to be a patient: *The ship sank; The ice is melting; This bikini washes easily*. In the PASSIVE VOICE, the subject is commonly a patient: *Mike was stung by a bee; The Arndale Centre was bombed by the IRA*. See also AGENT.

perfect The English construction consisting of the auxiliary verb *have* followed by the PAST PARTICIPLE of a lexical verb. When *have* is in the present tense, the result is the PRESENT PERFECT; when *have* is in the past tense, the result is the PAST PERFECT. See these two entries. Most commonly, the perfect represents a state of affairs resulting from an earlier event, but it also has other uses.

perfect infinitive The traditional, but pointless, label for a sequence of *to* plus *have* plus the PAST PARTICIPLE of a verb. An example is *to have met* in *I would like to have met Napoleon*. The name is inappropriate, since such a sequence is neither an infinitive nor a grammatical unit of any kind. See INFINITIVE.

perfective The ASPECT form which indicates that the action of a verb is presented as an unanalysed whole, with no internal structure. English has no particular form for marking perfective aspect, which is the simplest of the aspect forms. In the past tense, the SIMPLE PAST is usual: *Susie washed the car; Susie sneezed; Susie bought a new house; Susie worked in London*. Compare imperfective forms like *Susie was washing the car* and *Susie used to work in London*, which do assign some kind of internal structure to the activity.

In the present tense, we usually use the SIMPLE PRESENT to express perfective aspect, though this is not the most frequent function of the simple present. Stage directions provide a good example: *Iago enters stage right*.

Commands and instructions usually also represent perfective aspect: *Wash your hands!; Cut along the dotted line*.

See IMPERFECTIVE for an account of how this differs from the perfective.

Note: the perfective should not be confused with the PERFECT. In spite of the unfortunate similarity of their names, the two are entirely distinct. Regrettably, many books on English grammar do confuse the two, and you should be prepared to encounter this confusion in your reading.

perfect participle Another name for the PAST PARTICIPLE.

performance The actual linguistic behaviour which you exhibit on particular occasions. Performance is often imperfect, since we all suffer from slips of the tongue, mishearings, memory lapses and other shortcomings, but such slips do not result from imperfect knowledge of the language. Compare COMPETENCE.

period The American name for the FULL STOP.

periphrastic A label applied to a grammatical form which uses two or more words to express something which might, in principle, be expressed with a single word. In English, the label is chiefly applied to verb-forms constructed with one or more AUXILIARY verbs plus a lexical verb: *have eaten, is eating, will have eaten, has been eating, must have been eating,* and so on. But it can also be applied to two-word comparatives like *more lovely* (as opposed to *lovelier*). The use of a periphrastic form is periphrasis.

person The GRAMMATICAL CATEGORY which distinguishes participants in a conversation. Like most languages, English distinguishes three persons. The *first person* represents the speaker and possibly other people associated with the speaker. The PRONOUNS are *I/me* (singular) and *we/us* (plural). The *second person* represents the hearer(s) and possibly other people associated with the hearer(s), and the pronoun is *you.* The *third person* represents everybody and everything else, and the pronouns are *he/him, she/her* and *it* (singular) and *they* (plural).

personal pronoun Any PRONOUN which carries an expression of PERSON. The English personal pronouns are *I/me, you, he/him, she/her, it, we/us* and *they/them.*

phrasal genitive The English construction in which both the preposition *of* and a POSSESSIVE appear. Examples: *a friend of Susie's, those colleagues of mine.*

phrasal verb A complex verb consisting of a simple verb and a PARTICLE, like *make up, take off, turn on, do up* and *put away.* A phrasal verb differs from a sequence of a verb and a preposition (a PREPOSITIONAL VERB) in four respects. Here *call up* is a phrasal verb, while *call on* is only a verb plus preposition.

1. The particle in a phrasal verb is stressed: *They called* up *the teacher,* but not **They called* on *the teacher.*

2. The particle of a phrasal verb can be moved to the end: *They called the teacher up,* but not **They called the teacher on.*

3. The simple verb of a phrasal verb may not be separated from its particle by an adverb: **They called early up the teacher* is no good, but *They called early on the teacher* is fine.

4. The particle of a phrasal verb may not undergo PIED-PIPING: **The teacher up whom they called* is no good, but *The teacher on whom they called* is fine.

phrase A sequence of one or more words which forms a single grammatical unit. There are five principal types of phrase in English: NOUN PHRASE, VERB PHRASE, ADJECTIVE PHRASE, ADVERB PHRASE and PREPOSITIONAL PHRASE.

phrase structure Another term for CONSTITUENT STRUCTURE.

pictogram A more-or-less pictorial symbol which is intended to represent a word or a phrase without the use of language. In a pictogram, the idea is that the picture should suffice to convey the intended meaning directly, so that it can be understood even by someone who does not know the local language. Pictograms are common today in public places like roads and airports. For example, a sketch of a telephone handset means *Telephones This Way*; a sketch of a leaping deer means *Caution: Deer Crossing the Road*; a sketch of an airplane with its nose in the air means *Flight Departures This Way*; and a sketch of car tyre tracks zigzagging wildly means *Danger: Slippery When Wet*. Compare LOGOGRAM.

pied-piping The construction in which a PREPOSITION is moved to the front of its clause, just before its object. Examples: *To whom were you speaking?*; *With what did they hit it?*; *The shop from which I bought my gloves*. As can be seen, this construction is rather formal in English; the more colloquial equivalents are *Who were you speaking to?*; *What did they hit it with?*; *The shop (which) I bought my gloves from*, with PREPOSITION STRANDING.

place adverb An ADVERB that answers the question 'where?' Examples: *here, nearby, somewhere, above*. An ADVERB PHRASE that does the same is a place adverbial: *somewhere nearby, high above, right there*.

pleonasm The use of words which duplicate each other's meanings. Examples: *three a.m. in the morning, a free gift, his talents are not limited only to music*. Such a formation is pleonastic.

pluperfect Another term for PAST PERFECT.

plural That form of a NOUN which normally denotes that more than one thing is being mentioned. The English plural is regularly formed with the suffix *-s* (sometimes spelled *-es*): *girl/girls*; *ashtray/ashtrays*; *kangaroo/kangaroos*; *fox/foxes*. But a few dozen nouns form their plurals irregularly: *child/children*; *woman/women*; *tooth/teeth*; *sheep/sheep*; *millennium/millennia*; and others.

Not all nouns have a plural form: for example, *furniture*, *wheat*, *dust*, *drunkenness* and *silverware* normally have only a singular form. But do not confuse these with nouns like *sheep* and *deer*, which have both singular and plural forms. It is merely that, with these last nouns, the plural is identical in form to the singular: *This sheep is hungry*; *These sheep are hungry*.

There are also nouns with a plural form only; see PLURALE TANTUM.

plurale tantum A NOUN which is invariably plural in form, even though it may be singular in sense. Examples include *oats*, *cattle*, *remains*, *pants*, *scissors*, *binoculars*, *pyjamas*, *shorts* and *tweezers*. Such nouns are awkward to count: we cannot say **a pants* or **a cattle*, and we must say instead *a pair of pants* and *a head of cattle*. The plural of *plurale tantum* is *pluralia tantum*.

polar question **1**. Another term for YES-NO QUESTION.

2. Any question which offers a choice between two possible answers, such as *Are these units metric or Imperial?*

portmanteau morph A single linguistic form which clearly consists of two or more MORPHEMES but which cannot be neatly divided up into an obvious sequence of morphemes. For example, while past-tense *loved*, as in *I loved it*, can easily be divided (segmented) into a verb-stem *love* plus a tense-suffix -(*e*)*d*, the past-tense *took*, as in *I took it*, cannot be neatly divided up in the same way, even though it plainly consists of the verb-stem *take* plus the past-tense marker. Hence *took* is a portmanteau morph.

positive The basic, or dictionary, form of an ADJECTIVE. Examples include *big*, *pretty* and *enormous*. Compare COMPARATIVE and SUPERLATIVE.

possessive (also **genitive**) That form of a NOUN PHRASE which indicates that it represents a possessor. This is most commonly done with the SAXON GENITIVE *-'s*: *Susie's cigarettes, my mother's car, the students' work*. Some PRONOUNS take irregular possessive forms: *my family, their clothes*. But the possessive can also be expressed with *of*, especially when the possessor is not alive: we prefer to say *the legs of the table*, rather than *the table's legs*, even though we prefer *the horse's legs* to *the legs of the horse*.

possessive determiner A DETERMINER which expresses possession, such as *my, your, his, our* or *their*: *my wife, your mother, his new car, our old friends, their fate*. Though traditional grammar classes these as PRONOUNS, they are not pronouns but determiners, since they behave like determiners and not like pronouns.

possessive pronoun **1.** A PRONOUN which expresses possession, such as *mine, yours, hers* or *ours*: *This is mine*; *Yours is ready*; *as nice as hers*; *Ours doesn't work*.

2. The traditional, but inaccurate, name for a POSSESSIVE DETERMINER.

postdeterminer A label sometimes applied to a DETERMINER which follows another determiner within a noun phrase. Examples are *two* in *these two books* and *these* in *both these books*.

postmodifier A MODIFIER which follows the word or phrase it modifies. In the following examples, the bracketed items are postmodifiers: *warm* [*enough*], *too hot* [*to eat*], *tired* [*of London*], *persons* [*unknown*], *a better man* [*than I am*], *a yacht* [*big enough to sleep 24 people*].

postposition A word which is similar in function to a PREPOSITION but which follows its object. Basque and Japanese are two languages which use postpositions, as in Basque *Jonen kontra* 'against John' and Japanese *Tookyoo de* 'in Tokyo'. English has the postposition *ago*, as in *five years ago*, as well as *notwithstanding*, which may be either a preposition or a postposition: *notwithstanding this decision* or *this decision notwithstanding*.

PP The abbreviation for PREPOSITIONAL PHRASE.

predeterminer A label applied to the first of two consecutive DETERMINERS, such as *both* in *both these books* and *all* in *all my children.*

predicate That part of the sentence which is not the SUBJECT, the part that contains the VERB and consists of a VERB PHRASE. In the following examples, the bracketed portion is the predicate: *My sister* [*is a nurse*]; *Susie* [*put the mayonnaise in the fridge*]; *The Red Arrows* [*often perform at public events*].

In a QUESTION or in another sentence involving FRONTING, the predicate may be discontinuous, or it may precede the subject: [*Who were*] *you* [*talking to?*]; [*Behind the President stood*] *a row of bodyguards*; [*Seldom have*] *I* [*seen such a mess*]. Compare *You* [*were talking to Mike*]; *A row of bodyguards* [*stood behind the President*]; *I* [*have never seen such a mess*].

predicate complement A phrase immediately following a COPULA or a QUASI-COPULA. Examples (in brackets): *Susie is* [*a businesswoman*] (noun phrase; this is a PREDICATE NOMINAL); *Susie turned* [*bright red*] (adjective phrase); *Susie is* [*in the shower*] (prepositional phrase).

predicate nominal A NOUN PHRASE which follows a COPULA, one type of PREDICATE COMPLEMENT. An example is *a businesswoman* in *Susie is a businesswoman.*

predicative A label applied to a linguistic element which appears inside a PREDICATE. For example, the adjective *red* is in predicative position in *This shirt is red.* Compare ATTRIBUTIVE.

prefix An AFFIX which precedes the material it is added to. Examples include the *re-* of *rewrite* and the *un-* of *unhappy*. Compare SUFFIX.

premodifier A MODIFIER which precedes the word or phrase it modifies. In the following examples, the bracketed items are premodifiers: [*very*] *interesting,* [*nearly*] *finished,* [*straight*] *into the hole,* [*red*] *wine.* Premodification is the norm in English with most kinds of modifiers, but see POSTMODIFIER for a number of exceptions.

preposing Another term for FRONTING.

preposition The PART OF SPEECH containing words like *in, to, with, under* and *beyond*. A preposition usually occurs inside a PREPOSITIONAL PHRASE, but in some circumstances it may instead appear in the construction called PREPOSITION STRANDING.

prepositional adjective (also **transitive adjective**) An ADJECTIVE which can or must be followed by a PREPOSITIONAL PHRASE. Examples, in which the adjective is the first word in each case: *proud of Susie, frightened of snakes, ready for anything, concerned about this*.

prepositional passive In English, a somewhat unusual instance of the PASSIVE VOICE in which the grammatical subject is logically the object of a PREPOSITION. Consider the sentence *George Washington slept in this bed*. Here the verb *sleep* is intransitive, and *this bed* is the object of the preposition *in*. Nevertheless, this sentence has a corresponding passive form: *This bed was slept in by George Washington*.

Other examples of prepositional passives are *My flowers have been trampled on by the children* and *This bridge has been walked across by generations of lovers*. The circumstances in which the prepositional passive is possible are somewhat obscure. Many or all speakers reject efforts like these: **The garden was raced across by the dog*; **This tree is lived under by a fox*; **Susie is lived with by Mike*.

prepositional phrase (PP) A PHRASE consisting of a PREPOSITION followed by a NOUN PHRASE, its OBJECT. In the following example, all the bracketed sequences are prepositional phrases: [*After the game,*] *several* [*of the players*] *went* [*into town*] [*with their wives*].

prepositional verb See under PHRASAL VERB.

preposition stranding The phenomenon in which a PREPOSITION is left without a following object. The preposition *to* is stranded in each of the following examples: *Who were you talking to?*; *The woman you were talking to is my boss*. Compare PIED-PIPING.

prescriptivism The policy of describing languages as we would like them to be, rather than as we find them. Typical examples of prescriptivist attitudes are the condemnation of PREPOSITION STRANDING and of the SPLIT INFINITIVE and a demand for *It's I* in place of the normal *It's* *me*. Prescriptivism was a prominent feature of TRADITIONAL GRAMMAR, and it is still widely embraced today among non-specialists in linguistics. Linguists recognize the influence of prescriptivism in society, and accept some forms of prescriptivism as appropriate in educational contexts, but they reject it as a basis for describing languages. Compare DESCRIPTIVISM.

present The usual name for a TENSE category which includes reference to the moment of speaking. English has only two tenses, the PAST and the present; the present might better be called the NON-PAST, since it covers both present and future (English has no distinct future tense), as well as timeless statements. With most English verbs, the present tense is marked by the suffix *-s* in the third-person singular but otherwise has no marking at all.

The simplest form of the English present is the SIMPLE PRESENT, in which no AUXILIARY is present. This has several functions, among which the following are important.

1. It expresses timeless truths: *Rhubarb leaves are poisonous; Mongooses kill snakes; Water boils at 100°C; Viruses take over their host cells' DNA*.

2. It expresses HABITUAL actions: *Susie smokes; I get up at 7.30; The Danes drink beer; Susie drives to work*.

3. Especially in stage directions, summaries and the like, it presents an action as an unanalysed whole (this is the present PERFECTIVE): *Antonio enters stage left; Mercutio and Tybalt fight, and Mercutio falls; The white rook gives check, and black interposes his bishop*.

4. Especially in reports of intellectual debates or issues which are seen as currently relevant, it is used to present the views of scholars or writers of the past: *Grice presents sixteen maxims of conversation, but Sperber and Wilson propose just one; Hardy sees little reason for optimism in human affairs; Einstein assures us that no matter can travel faster than light*.

5. Especially in informal speech and in certain kinds of fiction, it serves to present a narrative with more vividness than that provided by the past tense: *This guy walks into a bar with a dog and asks the bartender for two beers; The mortally wounded Caesar slumps to the ground, his life's blood oozing out of him*. This function is often called the HISTORIC PRESENT, and it is hardly ever found in formal writing.

The present CONTINUOUS is formed by combining a present-tense form of *be* with the PRESENT PARTICIPLE: *Susie is eating dinner; The children are playing in the garden*.

The PRESENT PERFECT is formed by combining a present-tense form of *have* with a PAST PARTICIPLE; see that entry.

For the use of the present tense in referring to future time, see FUTURE. Compare PAST.

present participle The *-ing* form of an English verb, though only when this is not used as a GERUND or as a VERBAL NOUN. The present participle combines with the auxiliary *be* to form the CONTINUOUS aspect: *Susie is eating; Susie was smoking a cigarette*. It can also occur in a PARTICIPIAL RELATIVE CLAUSE: *The woman wearing the white skirt is Susie*. It also occurs in certain COMPLEMENTS: *I saw Susie crossing the street*. Compare PAST PARTICIPLE.

present perfect The English construction consisting of a present-tense form of the auxiliary verb *have* plus the PAST PARTICIPLE of a lexical verb. Examples: *I have finished the wine; Susie has quit her job; The UN has voted to impose sanctions on Iraq*. The present perfect is strictly a present tense in English, not a past tense, and it cannot co-occur with an adverb of past time: **I have seen her ten minutes ago*; **I have seen a good film last night*. The present perfect has several functions, but its principal function is to denote a present state of affairs resulting from an earlier action. For example, *I have finished the wine* means 'There is no wine now, because I drank the last of it earlier'. Compare PAST PERFECT.

preterite Another name for a PAST-tense form, such as *enjoyed* in *Susie enjoyed her holiday* or *took* in *Susie took her niece to the beach*.

primary auxiliary See under AUXILIARY.

principal parts Those inflected forms of a VERB which are required to construct all or most of its forms. In English, these are three: the INFINITIVE, the PAST TENSE and the PAST PARTICIPLE. For regular verbs, which exhibit the pattern shown by *love, loved, loved,* only the first is strictly necessary. Irregular verbs, however, require all three: *take, took, taken; write, wrote, written; sing, sang, sung; teach, taught, taught; put, put, put*. For the exceptionally irregular verbs *be, have* and *do,* even the three principal parts do not suffice to predict all of the irregular forms.

principles-and-parameters approach Another name for GOVERNMENT-AND-BINDING THEORY.

proclitic See under CLITIC.

pro-drop The property of a language in which a sentence does not require an overt subject. Spanish is a pro-drop language: it is perfectly normal in Spanish to say *Viene* to mean 'He/She/It is coming'. English is not a pro-drop language, and **Is coming* is not a grammatical sentence.

productivity The degree to which a grammatical pattern can be used freely to construct new instances. Productivity is most familiar in connection with WORD-FORMATION. For example, the noun-forming suffix *-ness* is highly productive, since it can be used to coin new nouns almost at will: *user-friendliness, sexiness, crash-worthiness*. In contrast, the noun-forming suffix *-th* (as in *warmth*) is not productive at all: it cannot be used to coin a single new noun, and **bigth*, **happyth* and **sexyth* are all impossible. Intermediate degrees of productivity are possible. For example, the adjective-forming suffix *-less* is of medium productivity: we can coin *braless, moonless* and *paperless* (as in *the paperless office*), but other formations, such as *forkless, cigaretteless* and *rugless* sound odd or worse to most people.

The productivity of a pattern can change. Until recently, the adverb-forming suffix *-wise* was unproductive and confined to a handful of cases such as *likewise, clockwise, lengthwise* and *otherwise*. But today it has become highly productive, and we frequently coin new words like *healthwise, moneywise, clotheswise* and *romancewise* (as in *How are you getting on romancewise?*).

pro-form Any linguistic form which has little or no meaning or reference of its own but which takes its meaning from another linguistic form present in the same sentence or discourse. See PRONOUN or PRO-VP for two important kinds of pro-form.

progressive Another term for CONTINUOUS.

prolepsis The use of a modifier which only becomes appropriate through the action of a verb. An example is *green* in *paint it green*, since the thing being painted is not green until the painting is completed.

pronoun The PART OF SPEECH which includes words like *you, they, somebody, anything* and *who*. A pronoun is one kind of PRO-FORM; it is usually a single word (occasionally two words in English), and it forms a complete NOUN PHRASE all by itself. Logically, then, the term should be 'pro-NP', but the less accurate label *pronoun* is established. Pronouns can be divided into several subclasses:

1. PERSONAL PRONOUNS (like *me* and *she*).
2. INTERROGATIVE PRONOUNS (like *who* and *what*).
3. RELATIVE PRONOUNS (like *who* and *which*).
4. INDEFINITE PRONOUNS (like *somebody* and *anything*).
5. DEMONSTRATIVE pronouns (like *this* and *those*).
6. REFLEXIVE PRONOUNS (like *myself* and *themselves*).
7. RECIPROCAL PRONOUNS (like *each other* and *one another*).
8. POSSESSIVE PRONOUNS (like *mine* and *hers*).

See these entries, especially the last, since the term *possessive pronoun* is often wrongly used.

As a rule, a noun phrase built on a pronoun cannot contain any other material: **the happy I, *the nice who* and **the other two anythings*, for example, are impossible. But there are a few exceptions: *little me, poor old you, what else, somebody nice, anything you like*.

proper noun A special kind of NOUN which is a name denoting a particular person, place or thing. In English, proper nouns are normally written with initial capital letters, and most proper nouns do not take an article. Examples: *Susie, Gwyneth Paltrow, Queen Elizabeth I, Dublin, Siberia, Never-Never-Land*. But proper nouns denoting historical periods and events, as well as certain others, often do take the article: *The Iron Age, The Industrial Revolution, The Meiji Restoration, The United States, The Hague*.

proposition The semantic content (meaning) of a statement. For example, the statement *Susie smokes* may be interpreted as saying 'The proposition *Susie smokes* is true', while its negation *Susie doesn't smoke* may be interpreted as saying 'The proposition *Susie smokes* is false.' Similarly, the YES–NO QUESTION *Does Susie smoke?* may be interpreted as meaning 'Is the proposition *Susie smokes* true?', and the WH-

QUESTION *Who smokes?* may be interpreted as meaning 'For which value of x is the proposition *x smokes* true?'

pro-sentence A single word which can take the place of a complete sentence. The most familiar English examples are *yes* and *no*. Here is an example. Jan: *Would you like some tobasco sauce?* Larry: *Yes*. Here Larry's response is equivalent to the sentence *I would like some tobasco sauce*.

protasis See under CONDITIONAL SENTENCE.

pro-VP A word or phrase which occupies the position of a VERB PHRASE but which has no meaning of its own, taking its meaning instead from another verb phrase, its ANTECEDENT. The two pro-VPs in English are *do it* and the more formal *do so*. In the example *I asked Susie to peel the potatoes, and she did it* (or . . . *she did so*), the pro-VP *do it* or *do so* is interpreted as *peel the potatoes*.

proximal See under DEICTIC POSITION.

pseudo-cleft See under CLEFT.

psych-verb A VERB expressing a psychological state, particularly one which, in English, is typically construed in the passive with a following preposition other than *by*: *be surprised at, be disgusted with, be excited about, be interested in*.

punctual The ASPECT category denoting an action which occupies only a moment of time. English has no special form for this. Mostly, we use the SIMPLE PAST for the purpose: *Susie sneezed; The bomb exploded*.

punctuation The conventional system of marks used in writing in order to display and clarify the structure of the text. The principal punctuation marks used in writing English are the FULL STOP, the QUESTION MARK, the EXCLAMATION MARK, the COMMA, the SEMI-COLON, the COLON, QUOTATION MARKS, the APOSTROPHE, the HYPHEN and the DASH. See these entries for summaries. For more information, see *The Penguin Guide to Punctuation*.

purpose clause A CLAUSE which expresses the purpose of an action. An example is the bracketed clause in the sentence *Susie bought a computer* [*so that she could work at home*]. For those linguists who recognize NON-FINITE clauses, the following example is also a purpose clause: *Susie is learning Spanish* [*to improve her job prospects*].

Q

quantifier A DETERMINER which expresses a concept of quantity. Examples are *many, every, most, all, some, no* and *both*: *many people, most students, no book, both cars.*

quantifier floating The construction in which a QUANTIFIER occurs later in its sentence than is logically required. For example, *All the students have passed their exams* is equivalent to *The students have all passed their exams,* in which the quantifier *all* has 'floated' away from its noun phrase.

quasi-copula A verb which resembles a COPULA but which has semantic content. English examples include *seem,* as in *She seems happy,* and *become,* as in *She became famous.*

question A sentence expressed in a form which requires, or appears to require, an answer: one kind of (functional) SENTENCE TYPE. Two common types exist: YES–NO QUESTIONS, like *Is Susie coming?,* and WH-QUESTIONS, like *Who were you talking to?* But other types exist, such as *Is that a snark or a boojum?* (This is a POLAR QUESTION.) These are DIRECT QUESTIONS, and they represent the INTERROGATIVE mood. But English allows utterances which have the force of questions, even though they have the form of statements, such as *You're coming with us?* (uttered with rising intonation). In contrast, a RHETORICAL QUESTION has the overt form of a question, but expects no answer. See also EMBEDDED QUESTION, TAG QUESTION.

question mark The punctuation mark [?], which marks a direct question. Example: *What are you doing?* For more on its use, see section 2.2 of *The Penguin Guide to Punctuation.*

question word Another term for WH-WORD.

Quirk grammars A series of grammars of English written by Randolph Quirk and his colleagues. Though rather traditional in orientation, these grammars are informed by contemporary linguistic research. They introduce a certain amount of novel terminology.

quotation marks (also **inverted commas**) The pair of punctuation marks [' '] (*single quotes*) or [" "] (*double quotes*). These are chiefly used to set off DIRECT SPEECH, as in the example *'Can I help you?' she asked.* See chapter 8 of *The Penguin Guide to Punctuation* for more on quotation marks.

R

raising Any construction in which a word or phrase which logically belongs in a SUBORDINATE CLAUSE appears instead in the MATRIX CLAUSE above it. See SUBJECT RAISING, OBJECT RAISING and NEGATIVE RAISING.

raising verb A VERB which can take a grammatical SUBJECT which is logically the subject of a following clause. A good example is *seem*. For example, the sentence *It seems that Jan is happy* can be expressed with the raised structure *Jan seems to be happy*, in which *Jan* has been raised from being the subject of *be* to being the subject of *seem*.

reanalysis A process in WORD-FORMATION in which an existing word is divided at a point at which historically no boundary exists, and one of the resulting pieces is removed and used to construct other words. For example, the word *hamburger* is historically derived from the city name *Hamburg*, but, in English, the word has been re-analysed into *ham* plus *-burger*, and the new element *-burger* has been used to coin further words like *cheeseburger*, *beefburger* and *vegeburger*.

reciprocal A form or construction which indicates that two or more people or things are acting upon one another in the same way. In English, reciprocal constructions are expressed with the RECIPROCAL PRONOUNS *each other* or *one another*. Examples: *Jan and I like to tease each other; The suspects have blamed one another for the crime*. Compare REFLEXIVE.

reciprocal pronoun A PRONOUN used in a RECIPROCAL construction. The English ones are *each other* and *one another*.

recursion The ability of a syntactic unit (a CONSTITUENT) to occur inside a larger unit of the same kind, and so on, without limit. Consider this sentence: *I'm reading a book about the reasons for the development of computers with the capacity for high-speed manipulation of virtual objects.* Here the prepositional phrase *of virtual objects* lies inside the large PP *for high-speed manipulation . . .*, which lies inside the PP *with the capacity for . . .*, which lies inside the PP *of computers . . .*, which lies inside the PP *for the development . . .*, which lies inside the PP *about the reasons . . .*

reduced relative clause (or **reduced clause**) Another name for a PARTICIPIAL RELATIVE CLAUSE.

reference The relation that holds between a NOUN PHRASE and the non-linguistic object or objects it picks out. For example, in the sentence *That cat has ruined my geraniums*, both *that cat* and *my geraniums* refer to particular things in the world. See COREFERENCE.

reference grammar A book providing an orderly description of the grammatical facts of a language, designed for looking things up rather than as a practical textbook.

reflexive Any construction which indicates expressly that two NOUN PHRASES in a sentence refer to the same person(s) or thing(s). In English, a reflexive sentence contains a REFLEXIVE PRONOUN. Examples: *Susie cut herself; Susie saw herself in the mirror; Susie doesn't know what to do with herself.* A few verbs intrinsically require a reflexive object: *Susie prides herself on her cooking; Susie perjured herself.* See INTENSIVE REFLEXIVE.

reflexive pronoun Any PRONOUN ending in *-self* or *-selves*. The English ones are *myself, yourself, himself, herself, itself, ourselves, yourselves, themselves*. The reflexive pronouns occur both in true REFLEXIVE constructions and in the INTENSIVE REFLEXIVE construction.

regular A label applied to any linguistic item which behaves in the way that is typical of items in its class. For example, the verb *watch* is regular (*I watch her, I watched her, I have watched her*), while *see* is IRREGULAR (*I see her, I saw her, I have seen her*).

relational adjective An ADJECTIVE derived from a NOUN which carries no meaning beyond that of the noun but which merely serves to provide a form of the noun which can be used as a modifier. Examples include *telephonic* from *telephone* and *Glaswegian* from *Glasgow*. English makes little use of these, preferring COMPOUNDS instead: we prefer *Glasgow telephone system* to *Glaswegian telephonic system*. Languages in which compounding is poorly developed, such as the Romance and Slavic languages, often make heavy use of relational adjectives.

relational verb A superficially TRANSITIVE verb which denotes a relation between two things, such as *have, own, involve, want, need* or *deserve*. Examples: *Susie has blue eyes; Susie owns a Volvo; Susie deserves more consideration*. Relational verbs are often difficult or impossible to put into the PASSIVE VOICE: **Blue eyes are had by Susie; *More consideration is deserved by Susie*. Note: relational verbs have sometimes been called MIDDLE verbs.

relative adverb An ADVERB which introduces a RELATIVE CLAUSE. The English relative adverbs are *where, when, wherever* and *whenever*. Examples of use: *The place where I come from is very small; The day when I met Jan was the best day of my life; I take my laptop wherever I go*.

relative clause (also **adjective clause**) A type of SUBORDINATE CLAUSE which is attached to a HEAD noun within a NOUN PHRASE. The most familiar type is a RESTRICTIVE (or DEFINING) relative clause, which is required to identify what is being referred to. Example: *The restaurant (which) we visited last night was pretty good*. Here the relative clause is *(which) we visited last night* (the RELATIVE PRONOUN *which* is optional), and it is attached to the head noun *restaurant* within the noun phrase *the restaurant (which) we visited last night*. This relative clause is restrictive, since it is required for identification: without it, we would have only *The restaurant was pretty good*, which does not identify the restaurant under discussion.

In contrast, a NON-RESTRICTIVE (or NON-DEFINING) relative clause is not required for identification, but serves only to provide additional information. Consider this example: *Margaret Thatcher, who hated trains, always refused to privatize the railways*. Here the relative clause is *who hated trains*, attached to the head *Margaret Thatcher*. This relative clause is non-restrictive, since it is not required to identify Margaret Thatcher: it merely provides extra information.

See also the special case illustrated under SENTENTIAL RELATIVE CLAUSE.

relative pronoun A PRONOUN which introduces a RELATIVE CLAUSE. The English relative pronouns are *who* (with its rare variant *whom*), *whose* and *which*. The complementizer *that* can also introduce a relative clause; when it does, it is counted as a relative pronoun by some grammarians, but not by all.

In most cases, the use of a relative pronoun is optional in English, and informal speech favours its omission. In the following examples, the optional relative pronoun appears in parentheses: *The woman* (*who*) *you were talking to is my boss*; *The coffee machine* (*which*) *I bought for my wife was on special*. In the following further examples, the relative pronouns *who* and *whose* are obligatory, and may not be omitted: *The settlers who jumped the gun in Oklahoma grabbed the best land*; *The creature whose bones we are looking at lived over 200 million years ago*.

Compare RELATIVE ADVERB.

reported speech Another term for INDIRECT SPEECH.

restrictive (also **defining**) A label applied to a MODIFIER which is required to identify the thing being talked about. Take the noun phrase *the old man*, containing the modifier *old* (an adjective). This can be used in two different ways. Here is one way. *A young man and an old man walked into the shop. The old man took off his hat.* Here, clearly, *old* is required to identify the man referred to ('the old man, not the young one'), and so *old* is a restrictive adjective. But here is another way. *The 83-year-old Sinatra was gravely ill, and it was clear that the old man did not have long to live.* Here, of course, the identity of the man under discussion is already clear, and *old* is not required to identify him, and so it is in this case a NON-RESTRICTIVE (or NON-DEFINING) adjective.

For examples of restrictive and non-restrictive relative clauses, see under RELATIVE CLAUSE.

retained object A traditional name for a certain NOUN PHRASE in a certain construction. In the sentence *My wife gave me this book*, it is far from clear whether the DIRECT OBJECT is *me* or *this book*. When this sentence is converted to a PASSIVE, the result is *I was given this book by my wife*, in which *this book*, whose grammatical role is now obscure, is the retained object.

rhetorical question A QUESTION which is asked merely for effect, and which does not expect an answer. For example, if I say to you *Do I look like a fool?*, then I don't expect an answer: I am merely choosing a rhetorical way of saying *I am not a fool*.

right-branching Any grammatical construction in which elements are added to the right-hand end of something which is already present. Right-branching is typical of English, and it is illustrated by the following example: *This is the cat that killed the rat that ate the malt that lay in the house that Jack built*. Compare LEFT-BRANCHING.

right-dislocation See under DISLOCATION.

right-node raising The construction in which two beginnings share the same ending. Examples: *Jan prepared, and Marian served, the sandwiches*; *She is a bright, though careless, student*; *By day the Americans, and by night the British, poured bombs onto Germany*. Rare in speech, right-node raising is typical of formal writing. It should be used sparingly, since it can be difficult for the reader to process. Note that, when written, this construction requires two commas, as shown.

root The minimal form of a LEXICAL ITEM (a dictionary word). In native English words, a root is usually identical to the independent form of a word. For example, the word *dog* always keeps the same shape in inflected forms like *dogs* and in cases of WORD-FORMATION like *doggie* and *doghouse*. But some other languages are different. For example, the Latin verb *amare* 'love' has the root *am-*, which appears in all forms of the verb, such as *amamus* 'we love', *amabit* 's/he used to love', *amavero 'I shall have loved'*, amare *'to love'* and amatus *'loved'*. Compare STEM.

rule A statement of something which is generally true in a language. In linguistics, we apply the term *rule* only to a statement of what we observe to be true of somebody's speech: for example, 'an English noun normally forms its plural by suffixing *-s*'. However, among the proponents of PRESCRIPTIVISM, the label is applied to a statement of somebody's opinion about good usage, such as 'You shouldn't use a split infinitive.' You should not confuse these two senses.

S

sandhi Any change in pronunciation, whether optional or obligatory, which occurs when two particular words or MORPHEMES occur consecutively. If the change occurs within a single word, we have INTERNAL SANDHI. For example, the negative prefix *in-* (as in *insane*) combines with *possible* to produce *impossible*. If the change occurs across a boundary between two words, we have EXTERNAL SANDHI. For example, the sequence *can't you* can optionally be pronounced as *canchoo*.

Saxon genitive See under POSSESSIVE.

scope That portion of a sentence which is included in the applicability of a QUANTIFIER or a NEGATIVE. For example, in *I didn't hide your vodka in the piano*, the negative has more than one possible scope, and the sentence is ambiguous. If the scope of the negative is *in the piano*, then the sentence means 'I hid your vodka, but not in the piano'. If the scope is *your vodka*, then the sentence means 'I hid something in the piano, but it wasn't your vodka'. If the scope is *hide*, then the sentence means 'I put your vodka in the piano, but not with the intention of hiding it'. If the scope is *I*, then the sentence means 'Somebody may have hidden your vodka in the piano, but it wasn't me'. To some extent, these different interpretations can be distinguished in speech by differing stress patterns.

secondary recategorization The phenomenon in which a word which normally belongs to one subcategory of its PART OF SPEECH is shifted to another subcategory, with different grammatical behaviour, with a shift in interpretation. For example, the English nouns *wine*, *coffee* and *intelligence* cannot be counted or pluralized in their central senses, but they can be counted and pluralized when recategorized to mean 'variety' (*Rhone wines*), 'measure' (*four coffees, please*), or 'embodiment' (*an alien intelligence*).

second person The PERSON category representing the addressee(s), and possibly also other people linked with the addressee(s). English, unusually, has only a single second-person pronoun, *you*. Many other languages have two or more second-person pronouns distinguishing number, sex, degree of intimacy, and other categories.

selectional restriction A limitation upon the ability of words to be combined which depends only on their meaning, and not on their grammatical nature. For example, *You have deceived my watermelon* is grammatically perfect, but it violates a selectional restriction: watermelons do not belong to the category of things that can be deceived. Compare SUBCATEGORIZATION.

semantic role Any one of several relations which a NOUN PHRASE may bear in its clause, classified from the point of view of the person or thing denoted by that noun phrase in the situation denoted by its clause, independently of its grammatical form. Among the most obvious semantic roles are AGENT, PATIENT, GOAL and INSTRUMENT, though many more are recognized by specialists. Any approach to grammar which places great emphasis upon the behaviour of semantic roles is a CASE GRAMMAR.

semantics The study of meaning. Semantics is not strictly part of grammar, but the dividing line between the two areas is often far from sharp.

semi-auxiliary A sequence of words containing a verb and having much the same function as an AUXILIARY but lacking the distinctive grammatical properties of auxiliaries (the NICE PROPERTIES). Familiar semi-auxiliaries include *have* (*to*), *be going* (*to*) and *be able* (*to*). Examples: *I have to go home; Susie is going to buy a new car; We won't be able to make the last train.*

semicolon The punctuation mark [;]. The semicolon connects two complete sentences when all the following conditions are met:

1. The two sentences are too closely related to be separated by a full stop (a period).

2. There is no connecting word which would require a comma, such as *and* or *but*.

3. The special conditions requiring a colon are absent. Examples: *Women's conversation is cooperative; men's is competitive. Tolkien published* The Hobbit *in 1937; the first volume of* The Lord of the Rings *followed in 1954*.

For more information, see *The Penguin Guide to Punctuation*, chapter 4.

semi-modal A conventional label for the two English verbs *need* and *dare*, which sometimes behave like MODAL auxiliaries but at other times like ordinary lexical verbs. For example, we can say either *I don't dare to do that*, in which *dare* is an ordinary verb, or we can say *I dare not do that*, in which *dare* is a modal.

semi-negative A label sometimes applied to an ADVERB which is not really negative at all but which behaves grammatically like a negative. Examples are *seldom, scarcely* and *hardly*. For example, *seldom* behaves like the negative *never* in cases like *Seldom have I seen such a mess* and *Never have I seen such a mess*, as opposed to the ordinary adverb *often*, as in *I have often seen such a mess*. In standard English, a semi-negative cannot occur together with a negative: *I can hardly see it*, but not **I can't hardly see it*.

sentence The largest grammatical unit whose structure is governed by rigorous grammatical rules. In English, a sentence always contains a SUBJECT (except in an IMPERATIVE sentence), and it always contains a PREDICATE. A sentence always contains at least one MAIN CLAUSE, and it may contain additional main clauses or SUBORDINATE CLAUSES. In writing, a sentence is written with an initial capital letter and a final full stop, question mark or exclamation mark. Examples: *The Vikings reached North America in the eleventh century*; *Who was the last Doge of Venice?*; *The students I've talked to tell me that they would prefer a takeaway exam*.

Sentences are variously classified; see SENTENCE TYPE.

It is important to realize that not every plausible UTTERANCE corresponds to a sentence: see FRAGMENT for examples of the difference. Speech makes heavy use of incomplete sentences, and informal writing may do the same. But formal writing normally consists entirely of complete sentences: this is one of the characteristics making it formal.

sentence adverb An ADVERB which does not merely modify a VERB or a VERB PHRASE, but which instead modifies the entire sentence containing it. Most commonly, a sentence adverb expresses the speaker's or writer's view of the likelihood, desirability or other characteristic of the state of affairs denoted by the rest of the sentence. Typical sentence adverbs include *probably, surely, certainly, undoubtedly, fortunately, unfortunately, frankly* and *hopefully*. Examples: *Susie will probably be coming* ('It is probable that Susie will be coming'); *Fortunately, Susie will be coming* ('It is fortunate that Susie will be coming'); *Surely Susie will be coming* ('I can't believe that she won't be coming'); *Hopefully Susie will be coming* ('I hope and expect that Susie will be coming'). Compare SUBJUNCT.

sentence type Any of the several types into which SENTENCES can be classified. If we classify sentences by their grammatical forms, there are four types in English: DECLARATIVE, INTERROGATIVE, IMPERATIVE and EXCLAMATORY. (These are traditionally classed as MOODS, even though English verbs do not vary for mood in the way that verbs do in some other languages.) If we classify them by their functions, there are again four types: STATEMENT, QUESTION, COMMAND and EXCLAMATION. Most typically, we use the declarative form for a statement, interrogative for a question, imperative for a command, and exclamative for an exclamation. However, we do not have to do this.

For example, *You will now sit down* has declarative form (it looks like a statement), but it can be used to issue a command. And *Boy, can Susie dance!* has interrogative form (it looks like a question), but it can be used as an exclamation. It is therefore essential, in classifying sentences, to distinguish form from function, since the two do not match up one to one in all cases.

sentential relative clause The construction in which a RELATIVE CLAUSE, instead of being attached to the HEAD NOUN inside an ordinary NOUN PHRASE, is attached to an entire sentence. Example: *The French and the Germans have refused to allow the sale of British beef, which has enraged British farmers*. Here the relative clause *which has enraged British farmers* is a sentential relative modifying the entire preceding sentence.

sentential subject The construction in which the subject position of a sentence is occupied by a complete sentence introduced by a

COMPLEMENTIZER *that* or *whether*. For example, *That Susie is drunk is obvious* shows the subject position of the main clause __ *is obvious* occupied by the sentential subject *that Susie is drunk*. See EXTRAPOSITION.

sequence of tenses (also **backshift**) A restriction on the choice of TENSE in a SUBORDINATE CLAUSE resulting from the choice of tense in a preceding MATRIX CLAUSE. For example, while we can say *Susie says that she is coming*, if we put the first verb into the past tense, we normally put the second verb into the past as well, producing *Susie said that she was coming*. Here *Susie said that she is coming* is somewhat unnatural, though not strictly ungrammatical: sequence of tenses is less rigid in English than in some other languages.

short passive See under PASSIVE VOICE.

simple past See under PAST.

simple present See under PRESENT.

simple sentence A SENTENCE which contains only one CLAUSE. Examples: *Susie will be here at eight o'clock*; *The King is dead*; *My brother-in-law wants to buy a new van*. Compare COMPOUND SENTENCE, COMPLEX SENTENCE.

singular The simplest form of an English NOUN, the form which is entered in a dictionary, such as *dog*, *tree*, *girl* or *spaghetti*. With a COUNT NOUN denoting a thing that can be counted, the singular is usually the form used to talk about exactly one of something: *one dog*, *a dog*, *that dog*. Here it contrasts with the PLURAL: *two dogs*, *those dogs*, *several dogs*. With a MASS NOUN denoting something that cannot be counted, the singular is usually the only form that exists at all, as with *spaghetti* and *flour*. But see PLURALE TANTUM for a class of exceptions. The GRAMMATICAL CATEGORY that distinguishes singular from plural is called NUMBER.

specifier A label sometimes applied to any grammatical word which specifies (delimits, identifies) the range of applicability of the phrase containing it. Consider the incomplete NOUN PHRASES __ *nylon shirt* and __ *nylon shirts*. We can complete these noun phrases by filling the blank with a DETERMINER which specifies something about which of all conceivable nylon shirts we have in mind: *a nylon shirt, the nylon shirt, this nylon shirt, any nylon shirt, some nylon shirts, most nylon shirts, all nylon shirts*, and so on. A determiner is therefore a specifier within a noun phrase.

Now consider the incomplete ADJECTIVE PHRASE __ *nice*. This time we can fill the blank with a DEGREE MODIFIER to indicate what degree of niceness we have in mind: *fairly nice, very nice, too nice, extremely nice, moderately nice, rather nice*, and so on. A degree modifier is therefore a specifier within an adjective phrase.

split infinitive A traditional but misleading label for a particular English construction. Consider the sentence *She decided to never touch another cigarette*. Here the sequence *to never touch* is an example of what is called a 'split infinitive'. Those who use the term believe that there is something wrong with separating the particle *to* from a following INFINITIVE like *touch*: they take the view that *to* is itself part of the infinitive, which they cite as *to touch*, and they object to breaking up this sequence with other material. But this view is quite wrong: the infinitive is a single word (here *touch*); the particle *to* is not part of the infinitive or part of the verb at all; and the sequence *to touch* is not a grammatical unit of any kind, as shown by the fact that it can be readily interrupted by other material.

stacking The 'piling up' of MODIFIERS. In the phrase *a pretty little white house*, the adjectives *pretty, little* and *white* are stacked on the head noun *house*, which is modified by each of them. In the more complex phrase *the finest Australian red wines*, the adjective *red* strictly modifies *wines*, while *Australian* modifies *red wines* and *finest* modifies *Australian red wines*.

standard English That particular variety of English which is regarded by educated people as appropriate for most types of public discourse, including most broadcasting, almost all publication, and virtually all conversation with anyone other than intimates. Standard English is the mother tongue of few people and is most commonly acquired only through formal education; consequently only the well educated normally acquire a good command of it. Standard English exists in both spoken and written forms, which at times may show interesting differences: for example, the form illustrated by *Much research has been done* is normal in standard written English but not in standard spoken English. Standard English can be spoken with almost any kind of regional accent, though some accents are regarded by some people as less appropriate than others for speaking standard English.

Standard English is not entirely uniform around the globe: for example, American users of standard English say *first floor* and *I've just gotten a letter* and write *center* and *color*, while British users say *ground floor* and *I've just got a letter* and write *centre* and *colour*. But these regional differences are few in comparison with the very high degree of agreement about which forms should count as standard. Nevertheless, standard English, like all living languages, changes over time: for example, standard English in the early nineteenth century required *My house is painting* and did not permit *My house is being painted*, while today it is the other way round. Because of this ceaseless change, there is at any given moment a noticeable degree of uncertainty and disagreement as to which usages should be accepted as standard. Here are some examples of usages whose status has recently been controversial: *She decided to never touch another cigarette*; *Hopefully we'll be there in time for lunch*; *I'm disinterested in opera*; *normalcy*.

It is important to realize that standard English is in no way intrinsically superior to any other variety of English: in particular, it is not 'more logical', 'more grammatical' or 'more expressive'. It is, at bottom, a convenience: the use of a single agreed standard form, learned by speakers everywhere, minimizes uncertainty, confusion, misunderstanding and communicative difficulty generally. But the social prestige of standard English is so great that mastery of it is now essential in a wide variety of careers.

statement The (functional) SENTENCE TYPE which expresses a proposition presented as true. A statement is normally made using the DECLARATIVE form: *Roses are red*; *Venus has no moons*; *I saw Mommie kissing Santa Claus*.

stative A label applied to a form or a construction which expresses a state of affairs, rather than an event. For example, *My window is broken* usually indicates a state of affairs (there is a hole in my window), and not the act of breaking the window. Especially in the past tense, English sentences can be ambiguous between stative and DYNAMIC interpretations. For example, *My window was broken* can be either stative (as in *My window was broken for a week*) or dynamic (as in *My window was broken by a hailstorm*); here only the second represents the PASSIVE VOICE.

stative verb A VERB which expresses a state of affairs, rather than an action or an event. Typical stative verbs include *know, want, believe, understand, fear* and *like*. In English, stative verbs cannot easily appear in the CONTINUOUS aspect: we cannot usually say **Lisa is knowing French, *Jan is liking Eric Clapton* or **I am believing you*.

stem In some languages, a form of a lexical item (a word) which typically cannot stand alone but to which affixes are added to produce word-forms. For example, the Latin verb *amare* 'love' has the root *am-*, from which are derived its several stems, such as the present stem *ama-* (as in *amat* 's/he loves'), the imperfect stem *amaba-* (as in *amabat* 's/he used to love', and the perfect stem *amavi-* (as in *amavit* 's/he loved'). Native English words do not usually make any distinction among roots, stems and word-forms. Compare ROOT.

stranding See PREPOSITION STRANDING.

strong verb A VERB which inflects by changing its stem vowel, such as *sing, sang, sung*. Compare WEAK VERB.

structural ambiguity An AMBIGUITY which involves assigning two (or more) grammatical structures to a string of words, as in *Visiting relatives can be a nuisance*. Compare LEXICAL AMBIGUITY.

structuralism An approach to describing the structure of languages which sees a language as an orderly structured system in which each element is defined chiefly by the way in which it is related to other elements. Structuralism was introduced by the Swiss linguist Ferdinand de Saussure in the early years of the twentieth century, and almost all approaches to linguistics since then have been structuralist. In the 1940s and 1950s, a particularly narrow version of structuralism was developed in the USA, and the term *structuralism* is sometimes used specifically to denote this kind of *American structuralism*. As a result, proponents of

GENERATIVE GRAMMAR sometimes use *structuralism* as a term of abuse for their predecessors, but, in the original sense of the term *structuralism*, generative linguistics is every bit as structuralist as its forerunners.

subcategorization The phenomenon by which the words belonging to a single PART OF SPEECH do not all behave grammatically in exactly the same way. Take verbs, and consider the following frames: (a) *Susie* __; (b) *Susie* __ *the cat*; (c) *Susie* __ *at the cat*; (d) *Susie* __ *me the book*; (e) *Susie* __ *she was coming*; (f) *Susie* __ *me she was coming*. Now try to insert the following past-tense verb-forms into the blanks: *smiled, chased, said, told, decided*. Quite apart from any awkward meanings that may arise, you will find that each verb fits into some of the blanks to make a grammatical sentence but not into the others. For example, *said* goes into (e) but not into (f), while *told* works the other way round. This is subcategorization: we want to assign all these words to the category *verb* because they all have important grammatical properties in common, but not all verbs behave in the same way.

All parts of speech exhibit subcategorization. For example, the preposition *from* can be followed by *under the chair*, as in *The cat ran out from under the chair*, but the preposition *to* cannot do this: **The cat ran in to under the chair* is not grammatical.

Compare SELECTIONAL RESTRICTION.

subject A particular GRAMMATICAL RELATION which may be borne by a NOUN PHRASE in a sentence. Most typically, the subject is the first noun phrase in the sentence and it represents the thing that the rest of the sentence 'is about', but this is not always true. Here are some typical examples, in which the subject is bracketed: [*Pratchett's Discworld novels*] *have sold millions of copies*; [*I*] *want to go home*; *Last week* [*a tropical storm*] *devastated Bangladesh*.

In the next examples, the subject is not the first noun phrase in the sentence: *This book* [*I*] *can't recommend*; *In the corner sat* [*a man in a dark cloak*].

In a sentence containing more than one CLAUSE, each clause has its own subject. Here is a simple example: [*Susie*] *told me that* [*Natalie*] *was ill*. Here *Susie* is the subject of the MAIN CLAUSE, while *Natalie* is the subject of the COMPLEMENT CLAUSE. The next example is more complex: [*The woman* [*you*] *were talking to*] *is my boss*. Here *you* is the subject of the RELATIVE CLAUSE *you were talking to*, while *the woman you were talking to* is the subject of the main clause. Hence one subject is contained within the other.

subject-attachment rule A rule of standard English by which the absent SUBJECT of a NON-FINITE phrase must be interpreted as identical to the subject of the higher clause containing it. Consider some examples: *Having finished her dinner, Susie opened a book*; *Before going out, Susie checked the back door*; *Wearied by the discussion, Susie left the meeting*. In all these cases it must be Susie, and only Susie, who finished dinner, who went out and who was wearied. Violation of this rule produces a DANGLING PARTICIPLE; see that entry.

subject control See under CONTROL.

subjective genitive A POSSESSIVE construction with *of* or *-'s* in which the possessed item represents the logical subject. For example, *Susie's arrival* is logically related to *Susie arrives*, and *the conquests of the Mongols* is related to *the Mongols conquered*. Compare OBJECTIVE GENITIVE.

subject raising The construction in which the logical subject of a subordinate clause appears on the surface as the subject of a higher clause. For example, in *It seems that Susie is happy*, *Susie* is both the logical subject and the grammatical subject of *be happy*. However, in the alternative form *Susie seems to be happy*, *Susie* has been raised to be the grammatical subject of *seem*.

subject-verb inversion See under INVERSION.

subjunct In the QUIRK GRAMMARS, a label applied to a kind of ADVERB OF ADVERBIAL which does not modify a verb or a verb phrase in the usual manner but which modifies the entire sentence containing it. A subjunct is thus rather like a SENTENCE ADVERB, except that it does not express the speaker's attitude. Consider the adverb *strictly*. In the sentence *She treats her children strictly*, the word is an ordinary adverb (an ADJUNCT in the Quirk terminology). We can ask 'How does she treat her children?' and get the answer 'Strictly'. However, in the sentence *Dogs are strictly domesticated wolves*, the adverb does not describe the manner in which dogs are wolves: rather, it means something like 'The proposition "Dogs are domesticated wolves" is strictly true.'

subjunctive A label for a MOOD distinction which was prominent in English many centuries ago but which is now almost entirely gone. In modern English, the ancient subjunctive, marked by distinctive verb-forms and expressing doubtful reality or unreality, survives only marginally. The distinctive subjunctive forms are now confined to the verb *be* and to the third-singular forms of other verbs; they are still common in American English, while in British English they are confined to very formal styles. A subjunctive normally only follows a verb like *suggest, propose, demand* or *insist*. Examples, in which the subjunctive verb-forms are bracketed: *I suggest that she* [*refuse*] *the offer; They are demanding that she* [*reveal*] *her sources; I insist that they* [*be*] *freed*. These subjunctive forms contrast with the corresponding INDICATIVE (ordinary) forms – in my examples, *refuses, reveals* and *are*, respectively. Informal and moderately formal British English in fact uses the indicative forms in all cases. British English therefore loses the distinction, still always made in American English, between *I insisted that they were locked up* ('I asserted vigorously that they were already in jail') and *I insisted that they be locked up* ('I demanded that they should be put in jail').

To avoid this ambiguity, British (and other) speakers sometimes insert the MODAL *should*: *I insisted that they should be locked up*. As a result, some grammarians extend the label *subjunctive* to sequences like *should be locked up*, but not everyone would accept this extended usage.

subordinate clause A CLAUSE which cannot stand alone to make a complete sentence but which must form part of a larger clause, its MATRIX CLAUSE. The principal types of subordinate clause are the RELATIVE CLAUSE, the COMPLEMENT CLAUSE, the ADVERBIAL CLAUSE and the EMBEDDED QUESTION.

subordinating conjunction (also **subordinator**) The PART OF SPEECH containing the words which can introduce an adverbial clause. These include *when, whenever, although, after, if*, and a number of others. See ADVERBIAL CLAUSE for examples of use.

subordination (also **hypotaxis**) The use of SUBORDINATE CLAUSES.

subordinator Another term for SUBORDINATING CONJUNCTION.

substantive An old-fashioned word for NOUN.

suffix An AFFIX which follows the material it is attached to. Examples include the *-ness* of *happiness*, the *-ly* of *slowly* and the *-th* of *warmth*. Compare PREFIX.

superlative That form of an adjective or an adverb expressing the highest degree. For *big*, this is *biggest*; for *bad*, it is *worst*; for *beautiful*, it is *most beautiful*; for *slowly*, it is *most slowly*. Compare POSITIVE, COMPARATIVE.

suppletion The use of two or more different stems to construct the inflected forms of a word. Examples include *person/people*, *go/went* and *bad/worse*.

surface structure In TRANSFORMATIONAL GRAMMAR, the overt outward form of a sentence; the form which it actually has when used. This contrasts with its DEEP STRUCTURE, which may be very different in form.

symbol Another term for LOGOGRAM.

synchronic Pertaining to a language at a given point in time, with no attention to the development of the language over time. That point in time need not be the present: we can equally construct a synchronic description of contemporary English or of Elizabethan English. Compare DIACHRONIC.

syncretism The grammatical phenomenon in which two functionally distinct forms of a word are identical in form. For example, many English verbs distinguish the PAST from the PAST PARTICIPLE: *I saw her*, but *I have seen her*. But *love* does not distinguish these two in form: *I loved her*, but *I have loved her*. This is syncretism.

syntactic category Any one of the structural categories of linguistic objects which can be used in building sentences. Among the syntactic categories are the PARTS OF SPEECH like NOUN and ADJECTIVE, and several larger categories such as NOMINAL GROUP, NOUN PHRASE, VERB PHRASE and even SENTENCE (since a sentence may contain a smaller sentence within it). See the example presented under TREE DIAGRAM. Compare GRAMMATICAL CATEGORY.

syntagmatic relation The relation between linguistic items which are present at the same time in the same utterance or sentence. For example, in the sentence *Susie bought herself a new suit,* there is a syntagmatic relation between *Susie* and *herself* (which refer to the same person) and between *bought* and *a new suit* (the second being the DIRECT OBJECT of the first). Compare PARADIGMATIC RELATION.

syntax Sentence structure, or the study of sentence structure: one branch of GRAMMAR.

Systemic Grammar (also **Systemic-Functional Grammar**) A particular approach to the study of grammar developed chiefly by Michael Halliday and his colleagues in Britain. Systemic Grammar is a variety of FUNCTIONAL GRAMMAR: that is, it attaches great importance not only to linguistic forms but also to the functions which they serve. Accordingly, its grammatical descriptions typically involve considerable appeal to the purposes which language-users have in mind, and its proponents have particularly stressed its usefulness in the study of TEXTS.

T

tag question A brief question which is tacked on to the end of a statement. English uses two different kinds of tag question, both of somewhat complex formation. Consider the statement *Susie is Irish*. One kind of tag question extends this statement so as to ask for explicit confirmation: *Susie's Irish, isn't she?* The other kind of tag usually forms only a RHETORICAL QUESTION not requiring a response: *Susie's Irish, is she?*

telic A label applied to a verb or a sentence which denotes an activity or state which has a recognizable goal whose achievement would necessarily bring the activity or state to an end. Telic verbs include *paint* (as in *Rembrandt painted* The Night Watch), *wash* (as in *Jan is washing her hair*), and *sack* (as in *The Mongols sacked Kiev*). The opposite is ATELIC.

temporal clause Any ADVERBIAL CLAUSE pertaining to time, such as one beginning with *when, whenever, after, before* or *while*. Examples (in brackets): [*When I was young,*] *television was in black and white*; [*After the French army was crushed in Serbia,*] *there was no effective Christian force between the Turks and the North Sea*; *I met my wife* [*while we were working in London*].

tense The GRAMMATICAL CATEGORY which correlates most closely with location in time. Like many other languages, English marks tense in verbs: *I see her* versus *I saw her*. English has only two tenses: the PAST tense and the other one, which is commonly called the PRESENT tense but which might more accurately be called the *non-past* tense or the *present/future* tense, since it generally expresses all times other than past time. Accordingly, the forms of English verbs usually come in pairs. Below are a few examples.

Non-past	Past
I see her.	*I saw her.*
I am watching her.	*I was watching her.*
I have met her.	*I had met her.*
I will visit her.	*I would visit her.*
I have been seeing her.	*I had been seeing her.*

If the relationship is not clear, try putting *I told you that . . .* in front of each. You should find that the past-tense form is far more natural than the non-past form in every case, because of SEQUENCE OF TENSES.

Unlike some other languages, English has no future tense. It is quite wrong to claim that forms involving *will* or *shall* are 'future': they are not future in tense merely because they often denote future time. See FUTURE for discussion. But some other European languages, such as Spanish, French and Italian, really do have three tenses, including a true future tense, and some non-European languages have more than three tenses.

tensed Another term for FINITE.

text A general term for any connected piece of speech or writing, such as a conversation, a lecture, a newspaper article or a book. Some linguists restrict the term to a piece of writing, preferring DISCOURSE for a piece of speech.

thematic structure The structure of a sentence seen from the point of view of the organization of the information it contains. The GIVEN AND NEW distinction is a familiar aspect of thematic structure, while TOPIC and FOCUS are others.

third person The PERSON category representing everyone and everything other than the speaker and the addressee and those people expressly linked with the speaker or the addressee. Practically all NOUN PHRASES are third-person: *she, they, the dog, my sister, Australian wines, Neptune, most first-basemen, beauty, the square root of seven,* and so on. In English, the only non-third-person noun phrases are the first-person pronouns *I/me* and *we/us* and the second-person pronoun *you*.

time adverb An ADVERB that answers the question 'when?' Examples: *tomorrow, soon, often, occasionally, always*. An ADVERB PHRASE that does the same is a time adverbial: *as soon as possible, next Thursday, whenever you like*.

***to*-infinitive** A traditional, but confused, label for a sequence consisting of the particle *to* followed by an infinitive. For example, in *Susie has decided to buy a new car*, the sequence *to buy* would be regarded as a *to-infinitive*. In reality, *to buy*, like other such sequences, is not an infinitive, nor is it a verb-form, nor is it a grammatical unit of any kind. See INFINITIVE and SPLIT INFINITIVE. Nevertheless, there is something of a tradition of using the *to-infinitive* as the CITATION FORM of an English verb, such as *to buy* for the verb *buy*. This somewhat eccentric use is not normal among linguists, is never found in dictionaries, and is not recommended.

topic That part of a sentence that names what the sentence is 'talking about'. Not every sentence has a topic, and, even in sentences that do have one, it may not be obvious out of context. Consider a simple example: Alice: *Where's Susie?* Mike: *She's in the library*. In Mike's response, it is clear that *she* (= *Susie*) is the topic, while the rest of his response is the COMMENT – that is, what is being said about her. See also TOPICALIZATION.

topicalization The construction in which a phrase is moved out of its ordinary position to the beginning of a sentence in order to serve as a TOPIC. Consider the following sentence: *I can't recommend this book*. It is possible to move the noun phrase *this book* to the front of the sentence in order to produce *This book I can't recommend*, in which *this book* is topicalized: that is, the new sentence is a comment about *this book*.

traditional grammar The name given to the entire body of grammatical description and investigation in Europe and North America before the rise of modern linguistics in the twentieth century. Traditional grammar is the kind of grammar that was taught in schools in the days when grammar was still taught in schools, and it is still the kind of grammar which is most often taught today in those few schools which teach it. While many of the insights and terms of traditional grammar have been accepted into contemporary linguistic work on grammar, others have been modified or rejected altogether as inadequate, while many new concepts and terms have been introduced.

Some contemporary work is still rather traditional in outlook, such as the QUIRK GRAMMARS, a series of grammars of English written by Randolph Quirk and his colleagues, but these works are none the less informed by more recent linguistic investigations.

transformational grammar An approach to the investigation of SYNTAX devised by the American linguistic Noam Chomsky in the 1950s, one version of GENERATIVE GRAMMAR. Transformational grammar is highly abstract and intended chiefly to serve certain theoretical purposes; it is not designed to serve as a framework for the practical teaching of language or of grammar, and it is not well suited to such purposes. For theoretical purposes, transformational grammar was largely displaced in the 1980s by Chomsky's newer GOVERNMENT-AND-BINDING THEORY.

transitive A label applied to a VERB which takes a DIRECT OBJECT. Some verbs are always transitive, and produce an ungrammatical result if used without an object. Among these are *destroy*, *assassinate*, *want*, *seduce* and *trigger*:

The Mongols destroyed Kiev.	**The Mongols destroyed.*
Sirhan assassinated RFK.	**Sirhan assassinated.*
Susie wants a new car.	**Susie wants.*
Susie seduced Natalie.	**Susie seduced.*
The bomb triggered an avalanche.	**The bomb triggered.*

Many other verbs can be either transitive or intransitive; see LABILE VERB. Compare INTRANSITIVE. The label *transitive* is also applied to a verb phrase or a clause containing a transitive verb.

transitive adjective Another term for PREPOSITIONAL ADJECTIVE.

tree diagram A pictorial way of displaying the syntactic structure of a sentence. Trees are widely used in the study of syntax, though proponents of different approaches to syntax may differ significantly in the way they draw their trees. The diagram below shows a typical tree structure for the sentence *The little girl hugged her doll*; the SYNTACTIC

CATEGORIES labelled are Det(erminer), A(djective), A(djective) P(hrase), N(oun), N(ominal) G(rou)p, N(oun) P(hrase), V(erb), V(erb) P(hrase) and S(entence).

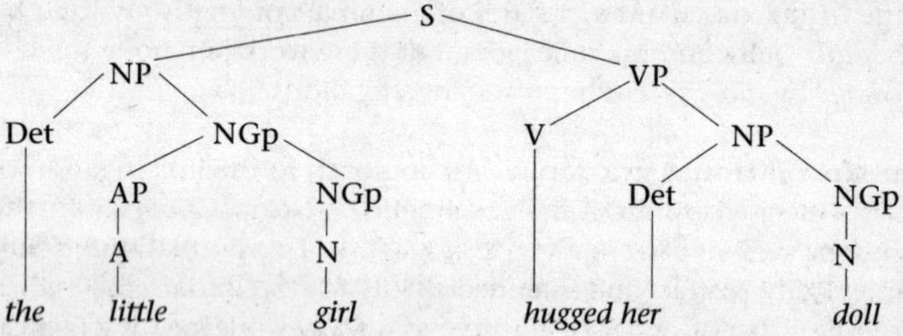

typology The classification of languages according to their structural properties, and not according to their ancestry. For example, in terms of ancestry, English is closely related to German and more distantly related to French, Russian and Greek, yet typologically it is in some ways rather more similar to the unrelated Chinese than to its relatives.

Chinese:	Gěi	wǒ	yī	bēi	júzishuǐ	ba.
	give	*me*	*one*	*glass*	*orange juice*	*OK*?

'Give me a glass of orange juice, OK?'
'How about a glass of orange juice?'

U

unbounded dependency (also **extraction**) Any grammatical structure in which an element of a sentence is removed from its ordinary or logical position and moved to the beginning of its sentence, possibly out of its clause altogether. Of the several unbounded dependencies in English, the formation of WH-QUESTIONS is the most familiar. The person or thing being asked about must be expressed by a suitable question word, such as *who* or *what*, and this word must be moved to the beginning of its sentence, no matter how far away this is from its logical position. Consider the following examples, in which the logical position of *who* is marked by *e*: *Who was Susie talking to* e?; *Who did Mike think Susie was talking to* e?; *Who did Natalie say Mike thought Susie was talking to* e?; *Who did Ted suspect that Natalie said Mike thought Susie was talking to* e? This can go on without limit in English: hence the name.

uncountable noun Another term for MASS NOUN.

underlying form An abstract representation of a linguistic form which is different from its surface form. For example, *won't* has the underlying form *will not*. A more elaborate example is *I can't seem to find my keys*, which may be said to have an underlying form of the approximate shape [*seem* [*not* [*I can find my keys*]]] – or, in English, *It seems to be the case that it is not the case that I can find my keys*. This last illustrates the meaning of the sentence more directly than the idiomatic surface form.

understood A very general label sometimes applied to any part of a sentence or an utterance which is logically required for interpretation but which is not overtly present, because its nature can be easily inferred from the context. Such elements arise in a variety of contexts; here are some examples. Alice: *Where's Susie?* Mike: *In the shower*. (Here *Susie is* is understood.) Alice: *Is Susie going to the concert?* Mike: *She doesn't want to*. (Here *go to the concert* is understood.) Mike: *Get yourself ready, Susie*. (Here the subject *you* is understood.)

ungrammatical Another term for ILL-FORMED.

unmarked form See under MARKEDNESS.

***un*passive** The English construction which looks in most respects like a PASSIVE VOICE, but in which the participle of the verb carries the prefix *un-*. Example: *Her arrival was unnoticed by the crowd*. This looks as if it ought to be the passive corresponding to **The crowd unnoticed her arrival*, but no such sentence is possible.

unproductive A label applied to a pattern of WORD-FORMATION which can no longer be used to create new words. An example is the noun-forming suffix *-th*, seen in *warmth* (from *warm*), *length* (from *long*) and *filth* (from *foul*). Today it is impossible to coin new words with this unproductive suffix: we cannot construct words like **bigth*, **sexyth* or **user-friendlyth*. Compare PRODUCTIVITY.

unspecified object deletion The construction in which an intrinsically transitive verb appears with no object, because the nature of the object is obvious or unimportant. For example, *smoke* can do this: we can say *Susie smokes Turkish cigarettes*, but equally we can say *Susie smokes*, in which the missing object is obviously 'cigarettes', or at least 'tobacco'. Other transitive verbs which can appear in this construction are *eat* (*Susie is eating*) and *read* (*Susie is reading*). The verbs which can appear in this construction constitute one kind of LABILE VERB. They are sometimes called ABSOLUTE TRANSITIVE verbs, meaning that they are logically transitive even when they appear with no overt direct object.

usage The manner in which a word or a construction is commonly used in a language. Descriptions of usage can be difficult, because usage in fact varies from region to region, from social group to social group, from person to person, and from context to context. Consequently, dictionaries of English, and sometimes also grammar books, frequently attach usage labels like 'chiefly American', 'informal', 'offensive', 'nautical', 'old-fashioned' and 'obsolete'.

A purely descriptive account of the language, as practised by professional linguists, will record and report those usages which are truly typical of the variety of English being examined (see DESCRIPTIVISM), regardless of what anybody thinks about them. However, an account of STANDARD ENGLISH, such as might be found in a textbook for learners or a guide to formal writing, must take a different tack: it must present those usages which are felt to be generally accepted as standard, and it must warn against usages not currently accepted as standard. But, since standard English – like every variety of every living language – is constantly changing, there will always be disagreements and uncertainties, even among specialists, as to which usages should be accepted as currently standard. This is why handbooks of good usage sometimes disagree with one another, and why they so often prefer to make recommendations rather than simply to lay down the law.

Here are two examples. Until the nineteenth century, the grammatical form illustrated by *My house is being painted* hardly existed in English, and the linguistic commentators of the day objected to it bitterly, condemning it as 'illogical' and 'monstrous', and demanding instead the traditional form *My house is painting*. Today, however, the once-offensive form is the only possibility in standard English, and no sane person would try to use the older form, which is now ungrammatical. Usage has changed.

Now, all contemporary handbooks of standard English will tell you to write *Shearer was replaced by Owen*, and to avoid the non-standard *Shearer was substituted by Owen*. However, observation reveals that the rejected second form is exceedingly common in the speech and writing of even well-educated people. In another generation or so, it may be that the authors of the handbooks will find themselves obliged to accept the second form as standard. That hasn't happened yet, but it may not be far away.

It is these ceaseless changes in usage which make it so difficult for us to decide just what exactly should be accepted as standard usage at any given moment. Since every new usage inevitably annoys some older or more conservative speakers, most handbooks will advise you to be conservative, to err on the side of caution, to avoid any usage, however widespread, which cannot yet be safely regarded as fully established in the standard language. But, of course, writers may genuinely differ on whether a given usage is now so established.

utterance A particular piece of speech produced by a particular person upon a particular occasion. It is important to distinguish an utterance from a SENTENCE, since an utterance very often does not correspond to a sentence. See FRAGMENT.

V

valency The number of ARGUMENTS required by a verb. A monovalent verb like *smile* or *sleep* requires only one argument: *Susie smiled*; *Susie was sleeping*. A divalent verb like *slap* or *see* requires two arguments: *Susie slapped Mike*; *Susie saw Mike*. A trivalent verb like *give* or *show* requires three arguments: *Susie gave Mike a kiss*; *Susie showed Mike her new kitchen*. Using a verb with the wrong number of arguments produces an ungrammatical result: **Susie smiled Mike*; **Susie slapped*; **Susie showed her kitchen*. But quite a few English verbs exhibit variable valency, such as *melt* and *swim*. Examples: *The ice melted* (monovalent); *The sun melted the ice* (divalent); *Susie was swimming* (monovalent); *Susie swam the Channel* (divalent). See LABILE VERB.

verb The PART OF SPEECH which contains words like *see, arrive, sleep, discuss, shoot* and *take off*. Verbs are distinguished from other parts of speech by a number of properties, illustrated here by the verb *drink*.

1. A verb can be marked for TENSE: *I drink wine; I drank wine.*

2. A verb can usually be preceded by an AUXILIARY: *I have drunk wine; I am drinking wine.*

3. A verb is the HEAD of a VERB PHRASE: *drink wine; drinking wine in the garden; drunk wine the night before.*

4. A verb can form a GERUND in *-ing*: *Drinking wine every night is bad for you.*

5. A verb can form a PRESENT PARTICIPLE, in *-ing*, and a PAST PARTICIPLE, usually in *-ed* or *-en* but sometimes irregular (*drink* forms *drunk*): *I have been drinking wine; I have drunk too much wine.*

Verbs are divided into two groups: LEXICAL VERBS (which includes most verbs) and AUXILIARIES (which have some special properties). Lexical verbs are further divided into INTRANSITIVE and TRANSITIVE verbs, with certain unusual intransitive verbs further distinguished as COPULAS and QUASI-COPULAS. The PHRASAL VERBS of English constitute a somewhat distinctive subclass of lexical verbs.

verbal noun A NOUN which is derived from a verb, usually by adding an AFFIX, and which exhibits all the ordinary properties of nouns and none of the properties of verbs. A verbal noun can be pluralized or counted (sense permitting); it can occur in a noun phrase with a determiner, with adjectives and with prepositional phrases, just like any other noun. In English, verbal nouns are constructed with a variety of suffixes: *arrive* (verb)/*arrival* (noun); *decide/decision*; *realize/realization*; *destroy/destruction*; *fly/flight*; and others. Examples, with verbal nouns bracketed: *Her sudden* [*arrival*] *startled us*; *These thoughtless* [*decisions*] *are ruining our business*; *I'm looking for a* [*flight*] *to Tokyo*. It is possible for a verbal noun to be unaffixed and identical to its source verb, as in *return* (verb)/*return* (noun) and *attack/attack*.

It is also possible for a verbal noun to be formed with the suffix *-ing* used to make GERUNDS, and such a formation should not be confused with a gerund, even though many textbooks make this error. For example, in *Deliberately bowling bouncers is unfair*, the subject NP *deliberately bowling bouncers* contains the gerund *bowling*, which, like any gerund, retains its verbal properties, such as the ability to take objects and adverbs. However, in *This deliberate bowling of bouncers has to stop*, the subject NP *this deliberate bowling of bouncers* is not a gerund but a verbal noun, as shown by its nominal properties: taking determiners, adjectives and prepositional phrases.

verb-complement clause See under COMPLEMENT CLAUSE.

verb phrase (VP) A PHRASE consisting of a VERB and all the phrases linked grammatically to that verb except a SUBJECT. Here is a simple test for verb phrases (VPs): *Susie* __. Any sequence which can fill the blank to make a grammatical sentence will probably be a VP. Examples: *smiled*; *was washing the car*; *wants to buy a mobile phone*; *has told me that she's getting married*; *will be vacationing in Jamaica*.

It is possible for a VP to contain a smaller VP within it. For example, the VP *was washing the car* contains the smaller VP *washing the car*, and the VP *wants to buy a mobile phone* contains the smaller VP *buy a mobile phone*.

The PREDICATE of an English sentence is always a VP, though VPs can also occur in non-predicate positions. In the sentences *Wanting to try on some bikinis, Susie looked for the changing room* and *Having made her choice, she headed for the cash desk,* the two sequences before the commas are VPs but are not in predicate position.

vocabulary The set of words known by a particular person. We must distinguish between your *active vocabulary,* the words you use yourself, and your *passive vocabulary,* the additional words you understand but do not use. Your passive vocabulary is always bigger than your active vocabulary.

The passive vocabulary of a typical moderately well-educated speaker of English has been variously estimated between 50,000 and 250,000 words. For comparison, a good desk dictionary of English typically enters around 100,000 words. Compare LEXICON.

vocative A NOUN PHRASE used to address someone directly. In the examples *Susie, come here* and *Where do you think you're going, young man?,* the NPs *Susie* and *young man* are vocatives.

voice The GRAMMATICAL CATEGORY which deals with the way the noun phrases representing the participants in an event are assigned to GRAMMATICAL RELATIONS. English distinguishes only two voices, the ACTIVE VOICE and the PASSIVE VOICE, and these are distinguished only with TRANSITIVE verbs. In an active sentence, the grammatical subject represents the performer of the action, while in a passive sentence the subject represents the thing undergoing the action, and the performer is either expressed with a *by* phrase (the long passive) or removed from the sentence altogether (the short passive). For example, the active sentence *The Mongols sacked Kiev* has the long passive counterpart *Kiev was sacked by the Mongols,* as well as the short passive *Kiev was sacked.*

VP The abbreviation for VERB PHRASE.

VP-deletion The construction in which a VERB PHRASE which would duplicate a preceding verb phrase does not appear overtly in the sentence. Example: *Jan wants me to get my hair cut, but I don't want to.* This is equivalent to . . . *but I don't want to get my hair cut,* with the second occurrence of the verb phrase *get my hair cut* deleted.

W

weak verb In English, a VERB which forms both its past tense and its past participle by adding the suffix -*(e)d*. Examples: *love, loved, loved; wash, washed, washed; smoke, smoked, smoked*. Compare STRONG VERB.

weather verb A verb which denotes some kind of weather phenomenon and which, in English, normally permits no subject other than the dummy subject *it*. The weather verbs include *rain, snow, sleet, hail, thunder* and *freeze*, among others. Examples: *It's raining; It snowed last night; It's thundering; It's freezing today*.

well-formed (also **grammatical**) Of a sentence, constructed in accordance with all the grammatical rules of the language. For example, in standard English, *I haven't finished dinner* is well-formed, while **I hasn't finished dinner* and **I ain't finished dinner* are not well-formed (they are ILL-FORMED). The last one, however, is well-formed in many non-standard regional varieties of English. The rules governing well-formedness are not the same in all varieties of English; see RULE. See also ACCEPTABILITY.

WH-cleft See under CLEFT.

WH-question A QUESTION which uses a WH-WORD and which expects an answer other than *yes* or *no*. Examples: *What are you doing?*; *Where did you find that?*; *Why are you crying?* Compare YES–NO QUESTION.

WH-word (also **question word**) A word which asks a question. In English, these words are *who, what, which, where, when, why* and *how*.

word A term with several quite distinct senses, which must be carefully distinguished. An *orthographic word* is anything written with a white space at each end and no white spaces in the middle: *snowed, grammar, can't, re-election.* A *phonological word* is any sequence pronounced as a single unit: all of the preceding four examples plus *ice cream, no one* and *take off.* A LEXICAL ITEM is an item of vocabulary, a word in the sense in which a dictionary contains words; see that entry for more information. A WORD-FORM is any one of the several different forms a lexical item may assume for grammatical purposes; see that entry for more information.

For example, *take* and *took* are two different orthographic words (they are written differently), two different phonological words (they are pronounced differently), one lexical item (they are both forms of the lexical item *take*), and two different word-forms (they are different grammatical forms of *take*). In contrast, *bear* (the name of the animal) and *bear* (the verb, as in *I can't bear this*) are one orthographic word (they are written the same), one phonological word (they are pronounced the same), two lexical items (they must be entered separately in the dictionary), and two word-forms (one is a noun, the other a verb).

word class Another term for PART OF SPEECH.

word-form The particular form which a given lexical item assumes in a particular context for grammatical reasons. For example, the lexical item *dog* can appear either in the word-form *dog* or in the word-form *dogs*: *That dog is dangerous*; *Those dogs are dangerous*. Likewise, the lexical item *take* can appear in any of several word-forms: *take, takes, took, taking, taken*. Examples: *Shall we take an umbrella?*; *Susie takes an umbrella to work*; *I took an umbrella with me*; *We're all taking umbrellas*; *You should have taken an umbrella*. Compare LEXICAL ITEM.

word-formation The process of constructing new words from the existing resources of a language. The most important processes of word-formation in English are compounding (see under COMPOUND) and DERIVATION. Other significant processes include BACK-FORMATION, CLIPPING, REANALYSIS, BLENDING, and the coining of ACRONYMS and INITIALISMS. See PRODUCTIVITY, and compare BORROWING.

word order The order in which words and phrases occur within a sentence. The BASIC WORD ORDER of English is Subject-Verb-Object, as in *Susie wrote this book*, though other orders are possible in special circumstances, such as *This book Susie wrote*. The order of words within phrases is generally fixed, however: we must say *this new book*, and no other order is possible: **new this book*, **this book new*, **book new this*.

XYZ

yes–no question (also **polar question**) A QUESTION which expects *yes* or *no* as an answer. Examples: *Are you coming with us?*; *Have you brushed your teeth?* In English, a yes–no question differs from the corresponding statement only in word order. For example, the statement *The Europeans have won the Ryder Cup* has the corresponding yes–no question *Have the Europeans won the Ryder Cup?*, in which the AUXILIARY *have* is moved to the beginning of the sentence; this is SUBJECT-VERB INVERSION (see under INVERSION). Compare WH-QUESTION.

zero anaphor See under ANAPHOR.

zero-derivation Another term for CONVERSION.

zero determiner A name given to the absence of a DETERMINER in certain NOUN PHRASES. Examples: *Susie, beer, French wines, contraband ivory, drugs, linguistics*. In the sentence *Susie always takes Australian wine to parties*, all three noun phrases have a zero determiner.